My Journey

Major General William B. Steele, U.S. Army (Ret.)

Title: My Journey
Author: William B. Steele
Editor: Magnifico Manuscripts, LLC
Cover Art Direction/Design: Shannon E. Coffey
Book Design: Shannon E. Coffey
Photo Scanning, Restoration, Retouching: Shannon E. Coffey
Medallion Cover Photos: Robert Coffey II
Remaining Cover Photos: U.S. Army, Aflac, and Olan Mills
Photos: Collection the Steele Family
Published by Magnifico Manuscripts, LLC (Matthews, NC)
www.magnificomanuscripts.com
First Printing March 2012 by CreateSpace

ISBN-13: 978-0615610023
Library of Congress Control Number: 2012904158

Printed in the United States of America

Contents

Preface

Without any doubt, the United States is exceptional; it is the greatest country in the world. I know this because I have lived or traveled in forty-eight different countries and have seen life under communism, socialism, and dictatorships. Having been born an American with the opportunity to pursue life, liberty, and happiness was a blessing and my journey through life has been a wonderful experience.

My generation lived during a significant time in history. When I was born in 1929, the United States was becoming an economic giant and world power. Yet it still offered a quiet, safe, relatively stable, small-town environment for cohesive family life. During my lifetime, Americans have experienced some radical cultural changes, along with rapid and phenomenal scientific and technological advances. This occurred at a much faster pace than those advances experienced by past generations. The United States became the most powerful of all countries and assumed a leadership role in keeping the peace and promoting the spread of democracy. It has been an exciting time to live in this world.

Along the way, I have known many interesting, helpful, kind, and loving people. They have all influenced my life in a positive way; some more than others. I realize this more each day. Perhaps it is because I am getting older and have more leisure time to reflect on the past. But also over the past decade, I have developed a close relationship with God and let Him control my life. In the process, I have drawn closer to those I love. This has provided increased happiness, peace, and satisfaction. These factors have made me very appreciative of my lifetime opportunities, friends, and family.

It is said that the past is prologue to the future. Consequently, I want to share with my family and the generations of Steeles yet to come what I have experienced in the wonderful life God has given me. In addition, I want to document the role that others have played in making my life so precious to me and provide information regarding the Steele family history. This knowledge will pass with me if I do not record it. I do not want that to happen.

So, come along with me on my journey.

Chapter 1
The Setting

"Don't you ever do that to her again!" my grandmother yelled at my father. She had just watched her daughter suffer through a long and difficult delivery process in an Atlanta hospital. I guess my father listened to her. I was an only child.

Being born on August 17, 1929, also made me a "Depression Baby." The Great Depression began that year. Banks failed, the stock market crashed, businesses closed, and many people lost their jobs and life savings. Times were tough. As a baby, I didn't realize that this would have a profound impact on me.

When the Depression started, my parents were living in East Point, Georgia (a suburb of Atlanta), where my father sold insurance for his father-in-law. In the early 1930s, they began to feel the economic pinch and decided to move to Lilly, Georgia, and live on a farm with my paternal grandparents. My grandparents had already returned to farming in order to make a living and grow their food if necessary.

★★★

The Steele family can be traced back to 1780. My great-great-great-grandfather, Thomas J. Steele, was born in Marion County, South Carolina, along the Lynches River. After growing up in that area, he married Jane Trainor and had two sons: Thomas J. Steele Jr. and Samuel James Steele.

Samuel was my great-great-grandfather. He lived in what is now Darlington County, South Carolina. Because early deaths were common during this time period, Samuel married three times: Mary Lula Finklea (who bore four children), Hannah Jane Hinds Harrell (who bore one child), and Henrietta (who also bore one child). One of his children became my great-grandfather, George James Steele.

Born in 1851 in Florence, South Carolina, George eventually married Hannah Alice Lucas. They had four girls and six boys, and one of them was my grandfather Wade Hampton Steele. He was named for General Wade Hampton—a South Carolinian who fought in the Civil War.

My great-grandfather George was a farmer, mill owner, and banker in Pamplico, South Carolina. I once told my wife, "Look at this photo of my great-grandparents at their golden wedding anniversary party. They aren't smiling. Life must have been really tough on the farm!"

While giving testimony at the murder trial of a neighbor, my great-grandfather died of a heart attack on September 25, 1924. His testimony is included in *A Piece of the Fox's Tail* by Katherine Bolling, a distant cousin of mine.

In the early 1900s, my grandfather, Wade Steele, wanted an alternative to farming so he enrolled in a business school in Macon, Georgia.

While attending a Methodist camp meeting with his classmate Asbury Forehand, Wade was introduced to a tall, attractive girl.

"Wade, I'd like you to meet my cousin, Dora Walton, from Dooly County," Asbury said.

Wade was in love!

Dora Alice Walton grew up with her four siblings in Vienna, Georgia. Her parents were Elihu Elisha Walton and Queen Edna Varnadow. Reportedly, Elihu served in Company F, 12th Infantry Regiment of the Army of Northern Virginia and was wounded during the Civil War.

After their marriage in 1905, Wade and Dora built a house on a farm that Dora inherited near Lilly. They had two children: my father, Wade Hampton Steele Jr., was born on August 2, 1907, and his younger brother, George, was born on November 28, 1911. Wade Sr. and Dora were a very compatible couple. He affectionately called her "Chux" for some reason, and she called him "my little man" since she was several inches taller than he was. In 1915 they relocated to Pamplico.

My father went to college in Clemson, South Carolina. He was a slim, nice-looking man with black hair that formed a widow's peak in the front. Although short (about five feet eight inches), he was very athletic, loved sports, and played baseball at school.

One day, he began experiencing severe stomach pains and had an appendectomy. He recuperated at home and was introduced to his brother's English teacher, Lucille Berry. Just like my grandfather, my father met his wife through a chance introduction.

My mother, Francis Lucille Berry, was born in East Point on January 18, 1906. She was the daughter of Henry Smith Berry, a successful businessman, and Francis Elizabeth Lieupo.

My mother often joked, "My father married my mother because she looked as if she could bear lots of children. It was not for her good looks."

They had six children. All were handsome, getting most of their genes from a tall, well-built father who had dark eyes, a strong chin, and wavy brown hair.

Lucille Berry lived in a brick home with her five siblings. She was a slim, pretty, brown-haired woman about five feet three inches tall. My mother was also very intelligent, skipping one grade in high school and finishing college at Wesleyan in Macon at the age of nineteen. She then accepted a position teaching high school English and French in the small town of Pamplico where the impromptu meeting of my father changed her life.

After a short courtship, they were married on July 15, 1926, in East Point. Wade did not return to college. Instead, he worked for his father-in-law, Henry Berry, at his insurance agency until economic necessity caused them to choose life on the farm with my paternal grandparents in Lilly. Wade Sr. and Dora had already chosen to move from the business world back to farming. But rather than move to the Steele family farm in Pamplico, Wade Sr. chose to return to the wooden framed house in Lilly that he and Dora had lived in shortly after their marriage. Now their son was bringing his family to join them. The Steele family was together again. Like other strong American families during that time, they took care of each other and did not depend on the U.S. government for their necessities.

*My great-great-grandfather Samuel James Steele
and his wife, Mary Lulu Finklea.*

My great-grandfather George James
Steele and his wife, Hannah Alice Lucas.

My grandfather Wade Hampton Steele
Sr. and his wife, Dora Alice Steele.

My maternal grandfather, Henry Smith Berry.

My father, Wade Hampton Steele Jr.

My mother, Francis Lucille Berry.

CHAPTER 2

The Early Years: 1929–1942

The quality of life in rural south Georgia in 1929 was austere compared to city life in 1929 or current rural life. Accustomed to the city, my mother adapted and made the best of living on a farm with her in-laws. This meant living without electricity, plumbing, telephone, and central heating. Instead, kerosene lamps, well water, slop jars, outhouses, fireplaces, and wood-burning stoves were used. Mule-drawn plows and wagons were the norm; trucks and tractors were not yet common on farms. Few roads were paved. However, our family had each other, a roof over our heads, enough to eat from our crops, and a healthy environment for a growing boy.

My personal recollections began when I was about four years old. I fondly remember my grandfather "Da Da." He was larger than my father, especially around the middle, so he looked big from my vantage point. His head was bald except on the sides, and he usually wore a brimmed hat.

Once or twice a week he called me. "Let's go to the general store."

How I loved going with him! I sat on the counter and listened to his friends discuss the news of the day, address farming concerns, and poke fun at each other. Everyone respected my grandfather and wanted his opinion.

I usually received a treat. He gave me five cents for a cold drink and said, "But it can't be a Coke." Cokes were considered a drug.

Although he was very serious and stern, my grandfather was a kind man with a dry sense of humor.

My playmates were usually the children of six black families who sharecropped the farm with my grandfather. We played marbles and had a good time pretending we were cowboys and Indians. I was usually the leader in our games, probably because I was white.

Yes, segregation was in its prime, even for my family. Yet my parents were good to all the people on our farm regardless of color. My father quickly helped anyone who needed money, transportation, or his influence to solve a problem.

However, separation between the races was evident. I first realized this one rainy day when I invited my playmates to come into the house to play. They would not come in and went home instead. I asked my grandmother, "Why didn't they come inside to play with me?"

She answered, "They can't come in the house unless they work in the house. They know the rules."

I had trouble understanding this—they were my friends!

Despite my age, I enjoyed a lot of freedom roaming on the farm. My love for the outdoors grew as I watched cotton harvesting, plowing, wheat grinding, cane syrup making, and hog killing. I was particularly interested in watching the local veterinarian work on the animals. I thought

I would be a vet someday (before I encountered chemistry and physics).

One of my daily chores was gathering chicken eggs. Surprisingly, this was not without peril. The group of wooden boxes where the chickens dropped their eggs was elevated several feet, requiring me to reach up and feel for the eggs. One day, instead of finding an egg, I grasped a snake that had been eating eggs. It was wet and wiggling!

I quickly withdrew my hand and ran back to the house yelling, "Da Da! Come! Come quick!"

My grandfather got his shotgun and soon killed the snake. I did not stick around to help him clean things up.

While my mother was teaching school in Lilly, I stayed with my grandmother "Nanny." She was good to me—very patient and understanding. She was a large woman—not heavy but large boned—and wore her long salt-and-pepper hair in a bun on the back of her head. I only remember seeing her hair down one time when she was preparing for bed.

I stayed by her apron strings as she moved about the house each day. She had a cheerful, outgoing personality. I vividly remember listening to her talk to me about manners, morals, and values in life.

She recited memory phrases such as: "Do unto others . . .", "A stitch in time saves nine . . .", and "Two wrongs do not make a right." She was a good role model. She always had time to sympathize with me or give me helpful advice.

However, I always looked forward to my mother's return from

school. She also was very good to me. I suffered from malaria quite often during the summer (mosquitoes were a real problem), and I remember her caring for me and reading *Heidi* and *Robinson Crusoe* by lamplight. Her voice was soft and soothing. I felt loved because she spent so much time with me, and I credit her with instilling in me a love of reading.

My mother became principal the year I started first grade. I had many kids to play with at recess and was very happy. I spent a lot of time with my cousin Ralph Busbee, who lived in town with his five sisters. Ralph's grandmother and my grandmother were sisters.

Ralph and I were the same age, but there was little resemblance. Ralph was tall with dark hair and skin. I was shorter, with brown hair and fair skin. After school, we got a snack at his house or his grand-mother's house across the street. There was always something to eat in the screened kitchen cabinet where leftovers from the noon meal (dinner) were stored for the evening meal (supper). Our favorite snack was a cornbread muffin with sugar cane syrup poured into a hole we punched in the side of it.

Ralph and I had many opportunities to learn, try various things, and experiment. Since most men smoked, we decided to try it. However, we could not buy cigarettes or cigarette-making material and did not dare take any of our fathers' for fear of being caught.

When we were six, we picked two cigarette butts off the ground in front of the general store, took them to the outhouse, hid behind it, and lit the cigarettes. Our experiment was short-lived.

My grandfather went to the outhouse and caught us in the act. He looked at Ralph and quietly said, "Go home."

I knew I was in big trouble.

He led me to the car and spanked me. The worst part of my punishment was the guilty feeling I had on the silent trip back home.

Although he was firm with me, I loved my grandfather and jumped at every chance to go somewhere with him. He made me feel important and I emulated him in many ways with one exception—the way he dressed for bed. He always wore a long, white nightshirt. In the winter, he knotted a white handkerchief at each corner and wore it like a cap to keep his bald head warm.

My father was also firm with me, even though he was not home as often as my mother or grandparents.

One day during hog-killing season, I complained, "Do I have to eat hog again today?"

He responded, "You are being unappreciative and ungrateful." He explained in detail how we had to either consume the hog meat, salt, cure, and smoke it, or give it away before it had time to spoil. (We didn't have refrigerators or freezers at the time.)

I apologized and said, "I know I should be grateful. I'm just so tired of eating hog!"

Another time, I refused to take castor oil for a stomach ache and ran into a cotton field to hide since the cotton was taller than me. My father took his time looking up and down the long rows. When he eventually found me, he didn't say a word. He picked me up and carried me back to the house. I had my first application of his leather belt that day.

Occasionally, I didn't need my dad or grandfather for punishment. I once ate an entire bowl of leftover banana pudding. I got sick—sick—sick!

Because of the distance and the miles of unpaved roads, we rarely visited the Berrys in Atlanta or the Steeles in Pamplico. However, I do remember playing hide and seek with my Aunt LaRue in East Point. She wore a long fur coat and hid in a closet. When I opened the door, she jumped out. I ran away and screamed, "Mom! I'm being attacked by a bear!"

Every meal we ate while visiting in Pamplico included rice prepared in some way. Since rice was grown in that area, it was plentiful. My favorite was rice pudding. I'm sure they felt about rice the way I felt about pork!

★★★

In the 1930s, the federal government created programs and agencies to energize the economy. The Farm Security Administration (FSA) was organized to regulate farm production and assist farmers financially. My father secured a job with this agency in the summer of 1935 and we moved to Fort Valley, Georgia.

Fort Valley was much larger than Lilly. While Lilly had about 100 people if you counted them on a busy Saturday afternoon, Fort Valley had about 2,000 people in addition to several streets with stores and a movie house. Life was good. Our house near the main street had electricity and plumbing. I had a bicycle and a dog, my mother had a spring in her step, and my father wore street clothes every day. My parents truly loved each other and openly showed their affection. My father's nickname for her was Fanny Lou (for Frances Lucille) and my mother planned her meals around his preferences.

We lived next door to a family with a lot of children. We played games like cowboys and Indians and kick the can. I don't recall having many toys since I was accustomed to pretending. For example, a cardboard box became a fighter airplane or racing car. A few more became a fort. I used a knife to make slingshots from a board and blow guns from hollowed-out bamboo shoots.

My father was transferred to the FSA office in Tifton, Georgia, in the summer of 1936. We left the peach-growing area for the tobacco-growing area. Tifton was another nice, small town, a little larger than Fort Valley. We had a larger house with two stories located on a main street leading into the downtown area. I walked across the street to go to school.

This proved to be tragic. As I was coming home from school one day, my dog, Spot, ran into the street to meet me and a car hit him. He died in my arms. I was devastated.

I played and biked with many playmates. We marveled at the tobacco auctioneers as they sold the flats of tobacco leaves. In the summer months, the strong smell of tobacco leaves permeated downtown Tifton.

I am surprised it did not deter me from starting to smoke later.

We left Tifton in 1938 and moved to Thomasville, Georgia, where we lived until 1940. This was a small town noted for its many beautiful roses. Consequently, it manifested a more pleasant fragrance than that of Tifton's pungent tobacco smell. It was a pretty town with towering oaks and shady streets. We lived in a single-story house close to the town center, and my bike took me everywhere. I got too careless with the bike once and took a nasty fall that resulted in a severe ankle sprain—one I still remember!

While in Thomasville, I saw Spanish moss on trees for the first time. I did not realize how close we were to Florida, or how different things were in other parts of the world—differences that became apparent in my later life.

It was also the first time I realized my father had a drinking problem. I knew he drank alcohol on occasion, but I had not seen any effects. I recall waking up one night and listening to him argue with my mother about coming home late after having a drink with friends. This was a precursor of things to come.

We moved to Athens, Georgia, in 1940. Immediately, the FSA transferred my father to Montgomery, Alabama, temporarily. After a few weeks, we joined him and lived in a rental house for the rest of the summer. I only remember a messy plum tree in the backyard and a mammoth swimming pool a short bike ride away. I spent most of my time at this city pool. My mother spent her time worrying that I might contract polio, which was prevalent at the time. (The vaccine had not yet been developed.) My mother and I moved back to Athens before school started in September, and my father soon followed. Mother was much happier when my father was with us.

While in Athens, I became a Boy Scout and received my first uniform. I also began to notice girls. They were hard to miss. We lived next door to a sorority house and they were always coming and going. Our house was a duplex with a dormer. I had an upstairs private room where I could put the radio under the covers and listen to *Gang Busters* after I was supposed to be asleep.

In Athens, I developed a work ethic. I got up at 5 a.m. for a morning newspaper route. I picked up my papers from the street corner, rolled and banded them, and put them in the bike basket. I rode my route before school and usually encountered problems—neighborhood dogs, steep hills, rain, or cold weather. Yet I persevered!

I felt grown-up and I suppose my parents thought so, too. They took a two-week trip to a Florida beach in 1941 when I was eleven years old and left me home alone with a charge account at the local grocery store. I had the house to myself. No one told me when to go to bed. What more could I want? I had fun! When they returned, I had trouble explaining why I charged so much at the grocery store for ice cream.

Most people can remember where they were and what they were doing when significant events occurred. When the Japanese attacked Pearl Harbor, I remember we were leisurely listening to the Sunday morning radio.

My parents were upset. My mother frowned and looked at my father. She began asking a lot of questions. "How can this be? Are we at war? What will happen? Will you have to go?"

My father looked at his hands as his face lost all color. "We will just have to wait and see."

I remember trying to understand the significance of all that was happening to our lives and our country. Like my mother, my first concern was that my father might have to go fight.

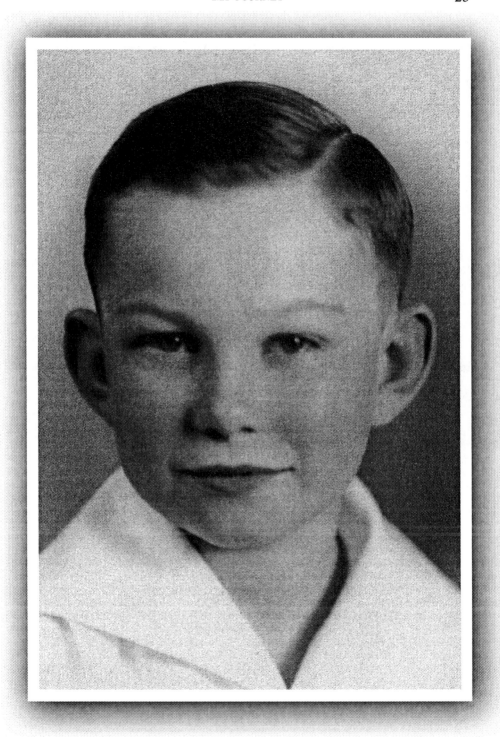

Me at age four or five.

With Grandfather Steele. "Da Da"

My parents in the early 1930s.

CHAPTER 3
Early Teenage Years: 1942–1945

In 1942 we moved to Lyons, Georgia. Lyons was a small town about five miles from the home of Vidalia onions—Vidalia, Georgia. We had a small, white, stucco house one block off the main street. A railroad ran straight through the town with the main street parallel to the railroad. I could walk to school, the movie, the drug store, and the grocery store. It was a great environment for a teenager, especially since teenaged girls lived on both sides of our house. Corky lived on the left side, and I spent a lot of time at her house. Her father offered me a part-time job at his grocery store. Weekly allowances were unknown to me, so having money in the bank was nice.

My mother went back to teaching school to make extra money for us. We were at the same school but did not see much of each other. Because of the war, efforts were made to improve the physical fitness of school children. We had daily conditioning exercises and a physical fitness course, including a wall to climb over, hurdles to go over and under, and a rope to climb. These challenged me, and I frequently stayed after school in an effort to master them—especially the wall climbing since it was higher than my reach. Little did I know that this type of conditioning would play a large role in my life.

By this time, the war was in full swing and there was an army camp nearby. On Saturday afternoons, off-duty soldiers filled the streets and the theater. This was my first contact with the military, and I was in awe of them. They looked sharp in their uniforms. Animatedly talking among themselves, they smoked cigarettes and had fun.

The summer of 1943 was eventful for our family. My grandfather, Wade Steele Sr., had gallbladder surgery in Macon. In the process, he developed peritonitis. He did not have the benefit of the antibiotics available today and died from the infection. He was in his sixties and had been in good health, so his death was a shock to our family.

This was my first experience with death in the family, and he was the only grandfather I had known. (My mother's father died of tuberculosis the year before I was born.) He, too, died early because of the unavailability of a vaccine or proper medication.

I vividly recall the events of his funeral, especially the two days he lay in state in our living room so that visitors could pay their respects. Relatives and friends sat up with him through the night. I stayed outside most of the daytime and certainly did not sleep well that night. I had not experienced having a dead person in the house, and it was a little scary. I looked at him only once. He did not look the same, and I tried to remember him as he was.

"Who can eat the most pancakes for breakfast?" he always asked with a twinkle in his eye.

"I can!" I responded. We'd both start eating, and he always won.

His funeral service was held in the Lilly Methodist Church, a church that had been a large part of his life. He was the first to be placed in our family plot in the Lilly Cemetery.

My father decided to take over operation of the farm and look after his mother. His brother, George, was living in Lilly with his wife's family, but he could not do it. He was paralyzed from the waist down because of a spinal infection contracted shortly after he got married. It was decided that George would handle the farm's finances and the paperwork; my father would do the rest.

Moving back to the farm and living with someone else did not appeal to my mother. I did not like the impending move at all. I was very comfortable in Lyons. My friends were there and the thought of life on a farm away from civilization had no appeal to me. It was with great reluctance that we left Lyons. The change did have one positive outcome for which we were grateful: farm products were important to the war effort, so farmers were deferred from the military draft. My father was exempted from the war draft.

We left the comfort of Lyons for the austerity of farm life in the summer of 1943. Fortunately, some lifestyle improvements had been made since we last lived there. The Rural Electrification Program had brought electric power to the area. Electricity also made it possible for water to be pumped from the well into the house. Therefore, we had a bathroom with plumbing, hot and cold water, and a toilet. In addition, coal-burning stoves had replaced fireplaces.

My friendship with Ralph Busbee resumed, and through him, I soon met other boys. My mother took a teaching job with Vienna High School for several reasons. My father did not have a fixed income from the farm, she wanted more independence, and she enjoyed the fellowship of teachers more than being at home with her mother-in-law and doing housework.

Normally I would have taken a school bus to the Byromville High School about four miles away. Instead, my mother informed me, "You are going to Vienna High School with me. It is larger and a better school than Byromville High. I know the importance of pre-college preparation, and this school has a better program."

When I started school, I recognized a pretty blue-eyed girl with long legs and blond hair. She was the stepdaughter of my Uncle Johnny Walton (Nanny's brother). I knew her from previous summers at Methodist camp meetings when we used to swim in the creek, eat large meals with the extended family, take naps after lunch (separately), and attend three church services daily. She was there with me when I professed my faith, became a Christian, and joined the Methodist Church.

I walked up to her and said, "Edna Claire! I need a friend here. Help me get started."

She smiled and exclaimed, "Billy! How great to see you! We will have fun at school together!"

We started attending school activities together and before long, we were going steady. This was okay because we were not related by blood. Before the end of the year, I became friends with several other girls and wanted to date some of them. I discussed this with Edna Claire, and she agreed that it might be best for both of us. We remained friends. Before long I found myself dating one more often than others. Her name was June Busbee. She was a nice-looking, considerate, out-going girl, and she was not related to me or Ralph.

The war affected many areas of our lives. Gasoline, sugar, butter, flour, meat, and various metals were rationed. Cars were no longer being built for civilian use. School athletic activities requiring traveling were stopped because of the gas shortage. Family outings were limited. We stayed at home and talked or listened to the radio together. War news was always desired. I recall hearing Edward R. Murrow with the news and found programs like *The Lone Ranger, Gang Busters,* and *The Green Hornet* entertaining.

Boy Scouts and school children collected paper, bottles, and tin cans that were needed for the war effort. The school's workshop and home economics building was used several days a week for canning food. Many people, including children, bought stamps toward war bonds. American civilians were involved in the war.

I learned very quickly that I didn't like farm work. I plowed weeds from rows of corn and cotton, stacked peanut plants to dry, and took cotton to be ginned. One very hot June day while plowing through rows of tall corn, sweating profusely, and following a corn-fed mule that was passing gas, I knew that farming was not for me.

It was not all work, though. Saturday and Sunday afternoons were free from farm work. If some family member was going into town, or if I could hitchhike to Vienna, I visited the drug store for a milkshake and then went to see a movie. You could usually count on a good Western picture show. Unless my folks were in town, hitchhiking was the way to get back to Lilly. I could walk home from there.

I was able to get a driver's license when I was fifteen years old. What a happy day! My mother taught me how to drive in a 1941 Dodge automobile. Now I could go places and take June out—our gas rations permitting.

I started working at the A&P grocery store in Vienna on Saturdays to earn spending money. One Saturday after June left for a summer camp in Chipley, Georgia, her good friend Virginia Nell Akin came into the A&P and spoke to me.

"June asked me to look after you while she was gone. So I came in to see how you were doing."

I smiled and replied, "I miss her, but I feel better now that I've met you!"

She came by a few more times during the summer. Virginia had hazel eyes and a nice smile that lit up her whole face. She was easy to talk with and I liked her, but we were just friends.

In the fall, I finally had my mother for a teacher in English. But my favorite class was chemistry. Virginia was in that class, and it was not long before I moved into the seat behind her. There was definitely some chemistry in this class! The teacher, Mrs. Lilly—yes, from Lilly—had trouble keeping us from talking during class and moved us apart several times. We managed to sit next to each other each day, and she finally gave up trying to keep us separated. Mrs. Lilly talked to my mother instead.

My mother gave me a lecture. "Don't let this friendship interfere with your schoolwork."

I don't think she approved, and she definitely was not amused.

By November, I worked up enough courage to ask Virginia to go to a football game in Cordele, Georgia, with me that coming Friday night.

She replied, "Let me think about it."

I was very nervous until I saw her the next morning. When she said yes, I was really excited. The weather was cold that night and it gave me a good excuse to sit close to her.

On the way home I told her, "I really enjoyed being with you this evening and would like to see you again."

She said, "Okay. I would like that, too." She smiled.

I was encouraged but did not press my luck and try to kiss her good night. As I drove to my house, I realized there was something special about Virginia. She was an attractive girl with dark brown hair, a slim figure, and very shapely legs. Watching her walk was a joy to me. She wore glasses that added to her looks. I liked to hear her talk—her voice was expressive and quite pleasant. Her grammar was correct, and she spoke with only a trace of a Southern accent.

I began to look for other opportunities to see her and was delighted when she started coming to school early each morning when the teachers had to be there. (She knew I rode in with my mother.) We sat on the school entrance steps and talked until classes started.

I needed to say something to June, and it was not easy for me to do so. One of my grandmother's memory phrases gave me courage: "The truth is always best."

Once my decision was made, I approached June. "June, we've had a lot of fun together and I know this is going to sound bad. But I really like Virginia, and I want to go steady with her. Please forgive me."

Virginia talked with her as well. I am sure that June was hurt, but she was very forgiving. Fortunately, our friendship with June weathered the storm and continued through the years.

For the rest of the school year, I spent as much time in Vienna as possible. For a while, I worked after school and on Saturdays at the A&P and later at Forbes Drug Store. Virginia worked around the corner at the dime store. We went to movies together and managed to have at least one date a week. Her parents were very strict and insisted that we double-date. Our double-date friends included Ralph and some of my other Lilly buddies. We had a great time together, going to juke joints and other places where we could talk, eat, dance, and just hang out. My mother

had tried to teach me to dance, but Virginia did a better job of it. The
Teen Club at school provided a supervised place to dance, and it probably kept a lot of us out of trouble.

Virginia's family originated near the Tennessee–Kentucky border.
Her mother, Oma Louise Shannon, was born in 1891 in Orlinda, Ten-
nessee, the daughter of William Edwin Shannon and Ollie Elizabeth
Brewer, who grew up on neighboring farms.

Reuben Claude Akin, Virginia's father, was born six years later in
nearby Mitchellville, Tennessee. He was the only child of John William
Akin and Queen Edna Barry. John William was a farmer, carpenter, and
horse trader.

Claude and Oma met while she was teaching in Mitchellville. Their
daughter Virginia was born on January 15, 1928, in Plant City, Florida,
where her father was working in a furniture store. When the Depression
came, he decided to become a mortician. He went back to Tennessee for
training and then relocated his family, along with his parents, to Vienna.

When I started dating Virginia, her family still lived in the large
brick house Claude Akin had purchased on Union Street in 1935 for
about $3,000. The Akin Funeral Home, located downtown, was built by
Claude's father, and it included living space for him and Queen to live in.
It soon became a thriving business. Depression or not, people still died
and had to be buried. Payment for services rendered, however, often
came late, was settled in trade, or just forgiven. Claude made a good liv-

ing, sent his children to college, and was respected in the community.

By spring, Virginia and I were going steady and considered our relationship as something that might last. She was to graduate that year and attend Georgia State College for Women (GSCW) in the fall. Her older sister, Helen, was attending GSCW, and her parents expected Virginia to study to become a schoolteacher. We dreaded the separation.

From the very first, I was comfortable with Virginia's family. Her parents were good to me and easy to talk with. They were much older than my parents and out of respect, I always addressed them formally. Mr. Akin was a short man. He wore glasses, was bald like my grandfather, and had an even disposition. Mrs. Akin was short, gray-haired, heavyset, and wore glasses. Arthritis caused her to limp slightly.

They readily accepted me and treated me as family. Having been an only child, I welcomed having a sibling relationship with Virginia's brothers and sisters. Ruth was an army nurse, so I did not see her until the war was over. Johnny worked for the Southern Railroad Company and was married and the father of Reuben and Shannon. Libby was teaching school in Richmond Hill, Georgia. Helen was at GSCW in Milledgeville. Virginia and R.C. were the only ones still living at home.

The Akins were practicing Christians who enjoyed church life. They were also talented. Oma, Helen, and R.C. played the piano well, and all members of the family had good voices. Amazingly, Helen could sit facing away from the piano and play the keyboard with her hands behind her back. Oma played the piano for church services, weddings, and funerals. For several years, the Akin Family Gospel Singers could be heard on the Cordele radio station each Sunday morning.

Virginia and I spent as much time together as we could. One Friday evening, I did something dumb. I actually ran away from home. I was looking forward to a date with Virginia and had been promised the car at 7 p.m. My father did not show up until almost 8 p.m.

"You promised I could have the car at seven o'clock and now I am late getting to Vienna."

My father yelled, "You are fortunate to be getting it at all!"

That did it. This had happened several times before, and I thought he had done it on purpose just to irritate me. I decided to leave.

I didn't have any money, transportation, or a place to stay. I had $12 from the Sunday School Fund (I was treasurer) and went away with only the clothes on my back. I walked the five miles to Vienna.

I called Virginia from a pay phone and told her, "I had an argument over the car tonight, and I am leaving home."

She was concerned. "Where are you going? What will you do?"

"I don't know. I am just going where hitchhiking will take me and be on my own. I will call you when I settle somewhere."

Then I started hitchhiking south on U.S. Highway 41 with no final destination in mind.

By morning, the rides I caught had taken me to Jacksonville, Florida.

I spent the morning looking around and tried to plan how I could get a job. The $12 would not last long, and I needed some clean clothes. I saw a sign pointing to the beach. *Why not get a look at the beach before looking for work?* Sounded like a good idea, so I caught a city bus.

While there, I decided to get a suntan. I took off my shirt and fell asleep on the sand. I woke up some time later with the start of bad sunburn on my back. It was getting late in the afternoon, so I went back to town to find work, food, and a place to stay.

No one seemed to want my services and by night I was beginning to feel the effects of my tanning experience. I spent the rest of the night trying to sleep at the rear entrance of a grocery store. The austere accommodations and the burning back did not make for a good night's sleep. By daylight, home seemed like a much better place. I started hitchhiking in that direction.

Amazingly, by late afternoon, I had reached Lilly and was walking down the dirt road to our house. As I rounded a bend in the road, I saw my mother walking in my direction. We saw each other at the same time, and we started running toward each other. We both cried.

The prodigal son had returned and was well received. My back was soon relieved. It was bathed with vinegar and then covered with flour. Unable to go back to school the next day, I rested and basked in the joy of being at home again. My folks had looked for me without success and called Virginia who told them of my call. The Georgia State Patrol was alerted. I had caused my parents, especially my mother, a lot of pain. I sincerely regretted my actions. I apologized to my father, and he did the same. Perhaps we both learned from the experience. (Running away from home may sound adventurous, but I do not recommend it.)

There was another time when I should have exercised more patience. At school during recess one day, I overheard Carlton Fowler say, "My English teacher is a horrible teacher."

He was talking about my mother.

"Take it back!"

"No! You can't make me!"

I decided to make him. Freddy Wehunt pulled me off of Carlton, but I think Carlton regretted his remark.

The principal and my mother both lectured me. My mother said, "You should not fight at school or any other place."

Yet I was not punished, and I felt justified in sticking up for her. I think she secretly appreciated my doing so. And no one made any more derogatory comments about her. Actually, she was a great teacher who was much loved. (Even today, when I see one of her former students, they tell me how much they learned from her.)

That summer turned out to be the best one I ever had. Virginia and I had many friends and we went on many dates—still double-dating, of course. My parents bought a tractor and an old but drivable pickup truck. Farm work was now easier and I had more mobility. I loved to go to town and pick up things for the farm. Whenever possible, I made a quick stop by Virginia's house. When I could time it right, I stayed for lunch.

During the summer, I learned it was not smart to hold the car door open while backing out of a car shed with exposed two-by-fours along the wall—the door would catch during the backing-up process. I learned a driver should not look too long at his girlfriend walking along the sidewalk. He won't see a car stopped directly in front of him, resulting in a bent fender. Trying to clean a dirty fender with Bon Ami was not a good idea either. The fender lost its luster forever.

I was at Forbes Drug Store with some of my Vienna friends one afternoon when the fire department siren sounded. Our farm truck was parked outside. I ran to it to go watch the fire. My friends followed and jumped into the back of the truck. Just as I turned the corner, the fire truck exited onto the street and turned in the direction I was headed. I followed behind them. The fire was not serious but my problem surfaced the next day. The fire chief told my father that I was following too closely and driving recklessly. I was directed to go to the police chief's office later that week for a judgment. In the interim, I anguished over what might be my fate. The fine turned out to be only $10 but the embarrassment was horrendous.

A baseball league was created in Dooly County that summer. Each town put together a team—Vienna, Unadilla, Lilly, and Byromville. My father managed the Lilly team. Having played baseball when he was in college, he knew how to coach. The teams played each other on Sunday afternoons. I played right field—or played at it. My cousin Ralph held center field. Although we had barely enough players to field a team, we held our own, even against the larger towns. I had a lot of fun and developed a real love for baseball.

Virginia learned to share my love for the sport. I picked her up in Vienna and took her to the game. She went to my house for supper afterward. She always helped in the kitchen and became friends with my mother and grandmother. She fit in well plus I happily drove her back to Vienna after supper.

Through baseball, Virginia also got to know my father. He loved to watch the minor league games played in Cordele at night. I went with him quite often, and we picked up Virginia as we went through Vienna.

My parents decided to send me to a military school in the fall to better prepare me for college. My mother did not think I was being challenged enough at Vienna High. In addition, my father had spent some time at a military school and thought I would benefit from a more disciplined environment. I went off to Gordon Military High School in Barnesville, Georgia, for my senior year. I had just turned sixteen, and I was about 100 miles away from Virginia.

Me at age fifteen.

Virginia Nell Akin at age sixteen.

CHAPTER 4
Military School: 1945–1948

Military school was a completely new world for me, but after the initial shock of regimentation and the consequences for any irresponsibility on my part, I found life there to be interesting and challenging. Except for missing Virginia and being a little homesick, I began to like it.

Life as a Gordon cadet in the first few months of the first year was difficult. From August until Christmas break, I had to stay on campus. I learned to be neat and orderly. I learned how to take orders, study, march, and endure extreme harassment without losing my cool. I was a plebe and a buck private without any privileges. I was called Steele, Private, or Bill. (I had the perfect opportunity to change my nickname from Billy to Bill since no one knew me from childhood.)

My roommate, Neil Radcliff, was a tall, lanky, towheaded boy from Akron, Ohio. He was a nice fellow despite the fact that he was a Yankee! Although most of the live-in cadets were from Georgia and Florida, there were boys from other states and several Central and South American countries. This was my first multicultural experience. Girls were also allowed to attend classes because Gordon was the only high school in Barnesville.

I now had an opportunity to participate in sports. I tried out for football but was not big enough to be on the line or swift enough to be in the backfield. I soon gave it up and tried boxing. One night I got into a fistfight in the barracks hallway with Ray Stallings, a cadet from south Georgia. Dr. R.D. Mohler, the in-house faculty member and coach of the boxing team, saw us from his apartment door and broke up our fight. He invited me to join the boxing team. He must have been impressed with the ferocity I had shown, because I did not have any boxing skills. I joined the team and fought in the welterweight class (147–154 pounds). I learned a lot but never enjoyed being hit. One season was enough for me.

When it was time for Christmas break, I was able to go home. I felt good about my achievements and wore my cadet uniform at home with pride.

Virginia and I spent a lot of time together during the holidays. I gave her a nickname by shortening her first name to Ginia (pronounced Gin-yah).

When the time came for me to return to Gordon, our parting was difficult. We were sitting on her porch and I had my arm around her.

"I don't want to leave you, Ginia."

"I know, Bill. I will miss you so much."

We comfortably sat in silence together. This was to be just one of many goodbyes for us in the years ahead.

When I returned to school, I was promoted to staff sergeant and became a platoon guide. In addition to the added responsibilities, I felt the pressure of my studies. My mother was right; I had been coasting at Vienna High. Fortunately, we had study hall from 7 to 9 p.m. each weekday night. Quiet prevailed, and monitors roamed the hall to ensure that we studied. My mother expected me to do well, and I did not want to disappoint her or waste the tuition. There was competitive pride at stake as well.

While the farm was paying my tuition, it was not providing any spending money for me. I waited on tables in the dining room. The work was easy but time-consuming. Nanny Berry also sent me an envelope containing a $5 bill at least twice each month—no letter, just money. She was great!

During the spring, I decided to lose a few pounds. Although not fat, I had gained weight and needed to trim down. With diet and more exercise, I lost weight, felt better about myself, and never let myself get overweight again.

The first year at Gordon went by very fast, with memories mostly of discipline and study. I walked the Bull Ring once to work off demerits for a minor infraction. I walked in a circle carrying a rifle for an hour at a time, directly in front of the administration building in sight of everyone passing by. This was embarrassing and tiring.

The cadets disciplined each other as well. One night my platoon leader blocked me from going into the shower room.

"Why can't I go in?"

He said, "Cadet Jordon stinks. He hasn't taken a bath in weeks. So we are giving him one." He smirked. "With a stiff brush."

We had several army officers and non-commissioned officers (NCOs) on the faculty to handle military instruction and training. I was impressed by Master Sergeant J.D. Dupree. He was a sharp soldier who had distinguished himself as a parachutist in World War II.

I asked him, "What's the best advice you can give me about being in the military?"

He replied, "Learn to improvise. You won't always know everything or have what you need."

I have found that to be good advice.

Graduation day came and I was very proud—I had made it through high school. My parents attended the ceremony.

Mother smiled. "I am so proud of you and thankful that we sent you here to finish school."

I couldn't wait to see Ginia. Conversely I was sad that I would never see some of my classmates again.

★★★

During the summer, I measured cropland so the FSA county office could verify crop acreage reports for subsidy payments. My pay was good and the map-reading experience was helpful. However, the work was dirty, sweaty, and tiring. Yet I was never too tired after work to clean up and see Ginia.

Frequently, I also accompanied my father to a baseball game in Cordele with a stop in Vienna to pick up our special passenger.

Unfortunately, my father's drinking was becoming more of a problem. It caused my mother to leave for a short time that summer. They argued, and she stayed with her sister in Atlanta. She told me she was leaving to give him an incentive to quit. They reconciled, but he continued drinking. He kept a bottle in a paper sack in his closet and would sneak a drink.

Suddenly it was September and time for me to go back to school. My parents and I decided I would attend Gordon Junior College for two years, and then finish at the University of Georgia (UGA) in Athens.

My responsibilities increased again when I returned to Gordon. I was promoted to company first sergeant and became the senior NCO in Company A. I supervised three platoons of cadets for formations, drills, and barracks' inspections.

The academic pace picked up. The college-level requirements—papers and lab work—kept me busy. Calculus, chemistry, and physics were difficult for me. Rather than fail calculus, I dropped out. I muddled through the other two, but it took a lot of time and effort. I realized that becoming a veterinarian was not a viable option for me.

My friend from Vienna, J.B. Ryner, started at Gordon that year. His mother told him, "Follow Billy's example. Go to Gordon! Discipline and challenging schoolwork will be good for you."

We roomed together for one year, but I was not much of a role model.

Because of my desire to see Ginia more often than Christmas and summer vacation, I started going to see her occasionally on weekends. This school absence was not permitted. Discipline was severe if one was caught. I left on Saturday morning after barracks' inspection, walked several miles to the Macon highway, and took a bus to Milledgeville. It was almost 100 miles. I arrived at the GSCW campus around mid-afternoon. Ginia and I walked around town or went to a movie. She had to be back by evening and could not leave the campus at night.

We sat and talked in the lobby of her dorm or on the campus grounds. I left by 10 p.m., caught a bus back to Macon, transferred to a bus to Atlanta around 1 a.m., got off at Barnesville about 2 a.m., and walked back to the barracks, hoping that the bed-checker had not noticed that the body in my bed was my laundry bag. Fortunately, my absence was not detected by anyone in authority. I still cannot believe I got away with it! Not everyone was so fortunate. One cadet, hitchhiking home from visiting a girl in Griffin, Georgia, got a ride with the wrong person—our commandant of cadets, Lieutenant Colonel Barnes Beavers!

In my second year of college, I was made a cadet officer. I was a lieutenant in command of a platoon of cadets in Company B and barracks commander of Powell Hall. My responsibilities and opportunity to learn increased again.

Apparently, Lieutenant Colonel Beavers did not think much of my military potential. While observing drill one morning, he reportedly told J.B. that I had a lot on the ball but would not go far in the Army—I didn't have a good command voice.

I guess it's good that J.B. did not tell me he said that until after I retired from the Army. Had he told me earlier, I might not have pursued a military career.

In spite of all that was going on that year, I continued to occasionally hitchhike to Milledgeville on Saturday and spend time with Ginia. She still could not leave the campus at night, so we sat outside on a bench—even on cold nights—bathed in the light of many security floodlights. I have often wondered why I took those chances; I was an officer and had a lot to lose. Love must have been clouding my judgment.

In the spring, things changed. Ginia came to Gordon for our spring parade and dance. This was her first contact with my school and friends. We had a good weekend, but I was beginning to have some doubts about our future together. Admittedly, I was being influenced by some of my friends who had been urging me to date other girls.

One friend said, "How are you to know if she is the one for you if you do not get to know other girls?"

I decided to follow their advice and told Ginia, "I still care for you, but I want to break off our relationship for a while. I am so sorry. Can you forgive me?"

She was hurt. "I thought you loved me. I thought you meant it. But if this is what you want, then I have no choice. I hope you are happy because I am not!"

I knew right then I had done the wrong thing. I felt like a heel and should have reversed the process. But for some reason I did not.

I dated other girls in Barnesville and at the start of summer vacation, I dated a few Vienna girls. I was missing Ginia, and no one else interested me. One night after dropping a date off at her home, I rode by Ginia's house and honked my horn. She heard it and thought I was flaunting my freedom. Then I found out she had dated a boy from Cordele. I was jealous. That it was a Cordele boy made it worse.

I showed up at her door one morning with "my hat in my hand" as my grandmother would say. Ginia looked through the open door without inviting me in. I didn't blame her.

"Ginia, I came to ask you to forgive me. I made a terrible mistake and want to have you back in my life. I miss you, and I do love you."

She let me come in and eventually forgave me; yet I do not think she ever forgot what I did to her.

Cadet lieutenant at Gordon Military College, 1947.

Spring parade at Gordon Military College, 1948.

Grandmother Steele "Nanny" and me, 1948.

CHAPTER 5

Marriage and a College Degree: 1948–1950

UGA was very different from Gordon. It was huge and spread out all over Athens, with thousands of students. I had to catch a bus to go to some classes. Several classes were large, and I felt like a very small fish in a big pond.

To make matters worse, finances did not permit me to live in a college dormitory or join a fraternity. Instead, I had a room in a private home owned by a woman and her adult daughter a few blocks from campus. I had a separate entrance but we all shared one bathroom. Food was another problem. I could not cook or keep food in my room and had no car. Fortunately, four of my friends from Barnesville were renting a house about two blocks away. Joe Smith had a Chevrolet convertible, and he was kind enough to let me ride with them when they went to eat at night. Breakfast was obtained on the way to class, and lunch was usually at the Varsity Restaurant across from the UGA main entrance. Weekends I was on my own using public buses.

On the plus side, there was no supervision and I was responsible only for myself. I decided to carry the maximum course load each semester to learn more and graduate sooner. I did not have much spare time, which was just as well.

When the second quarter began, I took in a roommate to reduce the cost of my room. He was a nice person but reflected the views and stringent restrictions taught by the Church of God. We had little in common, and when he dropped out of school before the quarter ended, I did not mind.

The university had a four-year Reserve Officers' Training Corps (ROTC) program. Upon completion, graduates were commissioned as an officer in the Army, Air Force, or Navy Reserves. Gordon College had provided me with the first two years in the army program; I could enter the university's program at the third-year level and on graduation receive a commission as a second lieutenant in the Army Reserve. This would be helpful in case of a future war. Moreover, it paid $27.50 each month of the school year. This was a no-brainer, and I signed up. That decision was to have a major effect on my future.

After a few weeks, I adjusted and settled into a routine. My studies were going well and I was feeling confident. Then, my love life took a turn for the worse.

Ginia was a senior at GSCW, accomplishing her practice teaching course in Eatonton, Georgia. Eatonton was only fifty miles from Athens. She was living in a boarding house with another student, Edwina Pearson. Therefore, it was easier to visit her and I did, whenever I could.

On one visit in January, she said, "I need to tell you something that you aren't going to like. I've started dating someone else."

I was devastated and gasped, "Why? I don't understand!"

She explained, "Edwina's boyfriend from Georgia Military College has a car and has been driving up to see her on weekends. He told Edwina that he would like to bring along a friend and asked her to see if I would go out with the three of them. I thought about it and agreed."

I asked, "How long has this been going on?"

She replied, "I have gone out with him the last two weekends."

"Are you doing this as payback for what I did last year?"

She said, "No, I like him. He is a senior at GMC and played on their football team last fall."

"How well do you like him? As much as you like me?"

"I don't know yet."

I was now on the receiving end and did not take it well. The trip back to Athens that night was long and sorrowful.

After many sleepless nights and much soul searching, I realized how much she meant to me and I set out to win her back. I called and asked to see her.

"I really want to talk to you about our future. Will you give me an opportunity to sit and talk with you soon?" She agreed to a visit the following Saturday. I spent the rest of the week planning what to say and do. I even bought a new sport coat to wear, along with a box of candy.

I was fortunate; the day was sunny and reasonably warm for a winter afternoon. Ginia was dressed in a skirt and sweater and looked very desirable.

I suggested, "Let's walk and find a place to talk."

Finding a little alcove with a bench that gave us some privacy, I asked, "Is this spot okay with you?"

"Fine with me."

My plea was simple. I grasped her hand, looked into her eyes and said, "I love you. I believe you love me; at least you seemed to for a long time. I believe our future is together. I acted badly last spring and I understand that may have led you to date someone else. But I have been miserable since our last visit. Ginia, I am here today, praying that you still love me and begging you—please come back to me!"

She thought for a little while and smiled. "Yes, I still love you. I'm willing to give us another try because I believe we have a future together, too." I returned to Athens that night a happy man.

Over the spring break, we started making plans. Because Ginia was eighteen months older and a year ahead of me in college, she would graduate in June. We could get married in August after my ROTC summer training camp. However, there were many "ifs": if my parents agreed to continue paying my tuition the remaining year; if she could get a job teaching in the Athens area; if we could live on the money she made and my ROTC pay; and if I could finish college next year. Only then would marriage be a possibility.

We needed to talk with our respective parents. My father would have to sign his consent for us to get a marriage license since I would not yet be twenty-one—the minimum legal age required for marriage.

My folks were difficult to convince; it was a hard sell. They didn't want me to get married so young. My father argued, "You can't support a wife. You can't even support yourself yet!"

My mother added, "You can't be sure she is really the one for you and what if she gets pregnant? You will not be able to finish college."

I continued to plead my case. "She is the one; I am sure. I will finish college; we have a plan. We are both sure this is what we want."

They finally agreed but with one additional if—if Ginia promised not to become pregnant until after my graduation!

Later, on a lighter side, my mother reminded Ginia that she was ex-actly eighteen months older than me, just as my mother was to my fa-ther—to the same specific months. "You can expect to be kidded by Bill about the age differential the rest of your life!"

Ginia's parents were somewhat difficult. They were sympathetic to our wishes but Mr. Akin told Ginia, "I will wait to give my answer when Bill asks me for your hand in marriage."

The traditional requirement was necessary to him, but it was not easy for me. I spent a lot of time dreading the process; fortunately, he did not drag it out or make it difficult.

I said, "Mr. Akin, I am in love with Virginia and I would like to mar-ry her."

He responded, "Will you take care of her and be good to her?"

"You can depend on it!"

He shook my hand. "All right, I give my permission."

With agreements by both families, the wedding plans took off!

Ginia's older sister, Helen, decided to get married that summer, too. Mr. Akin could only handle the expense of one wedding that summer, so a double wedding was planned. We agreed on a wedding date of August 7, 1949.

The ROTC summer camp enabled me to avoid most of the wedding planning and preparation, but the training was tough and stressful. We lived and were treated as army recruits, undergoing basic training with one difference—we were periodically rotated into different leadership positions. We were trained in individual skills such as weapons firing and map reading with a lot of physical training interspersed. We also conducted some platoon-level training

In one of the field exercises, I was a platoon leader, and we were moving through a thickly-wooded area. The head of our column came under fire, and I learned very quickly how difficult it was to maneuver troops under fire in wooded terrain. That training camp was a realistic experience of what being a soldier was like—seen from a private's perspective.

On returning to Vienna I was quickly caught up in the wedding activities, and before I knew it, August 7 arrived. I was too excited to sleep the night before. I was about to be married! I remember thinking, *Am I ready for this responsibility? Is she the right one?*

Yes. I was confident with my decision. I was in love with Ginia and wanted to spend the rest of my life with her. She was warm, friendly, well balanced, even tempered, cheerful, agreeable, and easy to please. She enjoyed the simple things in life and was very appreciative of even the smallest favors. She was capable of doing anything she set out to do. I enjoyed her company and felt that we would make a good team. Our marriage would last a lifetime.

The ceremony would not take place until 2 p.m. I had trouble containing myself. I bathed and shaved twice! At lunch, I received a few last words of advice.

My mother said, "Just remember the values you have been taught and practice them."

Nanny said, "Always put your wife's feelings first."

My dad said, "Be careful with my car." (We were using his 1949 Plymouth on our honeymoon.)

The day was one of the hottest days of the year. There wasn't any air conditioning in the church and it was packed with people. Several friends from Gordon were there, including my best friend Bill Smisson from Fort Valley. He and I had become buddies my last year at Gordon. Bill was one of my groomsmen; the other was R.C. Akin, Ginia's younger brother. Similarly, one of Ginia's bridesmaids was her college friend, Billie Jenkins. Fortunately she did not include Edwina Pearson!

My father was my best man. He was still a good-looking man. How-

ever, he had gained weight around his middle and his hair was beginning to thin, although the widow's peak was still prominent. (I inherited
that distinguishing feature from him.) While we were waiting, he assured me he had the ring and admonished me, "Don't drop it when I
hand it to you!"

I did not make that mistake, but my "I do" came out with more vol-
ume and conviction than I had intended and brought forth mild laugh-
ter. I must have meant what I was saying! Naturally some kidding
resulted.

Ginia was lovely. She was wearing a long, white gown with a lace veil
that framed her bare shoulders and her sweet, smiling face. She looked
at me with love in her shining eyes and I knew, without a doubt, she was
the one for me.

Because it was a double wedding, the ceremony was longer, as was
the picture taking. I remarked to Ginia, "The picture taking is longer
than the entire wedding."

Finally we joined the others already at the Vienna Community
House for the reception. As soon as the receiving line was finished, I told
my friends, "Off with the jackets!"

When it came time to leave, Ginia changed into her traveling clothes.
I had boasted to Ginia, "The car is well hidden from our mischievous
friends." I was mistaken. My friends found it in my Uncle George's garage and decorated it well. White chalk writing covered the windows,

ribbons hung from door handles, and a long tail of tin cans hung from the rear bumper.

The two of us needed an inexpensive honeymoon. We had only $200 from wedding gifts. But this gave us a few days at Daytona Beach. I stopped in Cordele to have the car washed, and we decided to eat there as well. We made it about fifty miles to Tifton before stopping for the night. It was a memorable day and a wonderful honeymoon.

Shortly afterward, we moved from my folk's house to Oglethorpe County near Arnoldsville, Georgia, where Ginia would teach school earning $112 a month. One of the conditions for her teaching job was that she had to live within the county.

Arrangements had been made by the school board for us to room and board with a couple who lived between Athens and Crawford. They were nice, but we had little in common with them and no independence. We had breakfast and dinner there, eating what and when they ate. We didn't have a car. They offered us a ride to their church each Sunday, but would not offer us a ride anywhere else. The husband drove past me on his way to work in Athens while I was waiting for a bus to Athens. When his wife complained that Ginia was washing clothes too often and running up their water bill, we decided to leave.

Ginia exhibited her resourcefulness. She convinced her principal to approve our relocation and arranged to ride with one of the other teachers who lived in Athens. We found a place we could afford with easy access to city bus service. It was a 288-square-foot porch that had been enclosed and divided into three small rooms: one for living, eating, and sleeping; one for a small kitchen; and one for a tiny bathroom. The sofa opened into a bed and the dinner table could be let down from the wall when the sofa was in an upright position. Without moving, I could wash dishes in the kitchen sink, then lean over into the bathroom and rinse them in the bathroom basin. It was not much, but it was only $57 per month. Most important, it was ours alone. We were happy.

During the last few months of college, I looked for a job without success. I was studying business administration with a major in marketing, and most of the available job opportunities were in sales. This meant being compensated on a commission basis. That did not appeal to me. I was looking for something more predictable and circumstances solved my dilemma.

I graduated on June 5, 1950, cum laude, and was inducted into two scholastic honor societies—Phi Kappa Phi and Beta Gamma Sigma. My grades merited magna cum laude but it required all course work to be completed at the university. (Since I had transferred in, I didn't qualify.) I received another honor at the Annual ROTC Military Ball. As commander of Company B, I escorted the company's lady—my wife—through the ceremonial row of crossed sabers.

Also in June 1950, the Army of North Korea invaded South Korea. The United States was at war again. On graduation, I was commissioned as a second lieutenant in the U.S. Army Reserve. But I had been selected as a distinguished military graduate and was given an opportunity to receive a commission and a career in the regular Army instead of the Army Reserve.

I had a choice to make and it affected my retirement: I could choose the Army Reserve, take my chance on my length of active duty, possibly retiring with fifty percent pay after twenty years of service; or I could choose the regular Army and have greater assurance of staying in and retiring with seventy-five percent pay after thirty years of service. In the latter case, I would be committed to stay in for a minimum of four years.

I discussed this with Ginia and our parents.

My father said, "I think the retirement provision is great! I regret that I don't have a retirement income to look forward to."

My grandmother agreed with him but added, "This means you could be living all over the world."

My mother liked the travel opportunities but lamented, "You may be in a war and you could be hurt or worse."

Mrs. Akin's view was negative. "From what I hear, army people are not the best class of people and they drink a lot."

Claude, on the other hand, said, "I think you should do what interests you."

As I expected, Ginia said, "It is your choice and I am willing to do whatever you choose."

I decided to accept the offer and pursue an army career.

The U.S. Army was not prepared for the Korean conflict. Its strength was drastically reduced following World War II. While the small active-duty force tried to delay the North Korean advance, the U.S. Army began calling units and individuals from the National Guard and the Reserve. At the same time, a number of infantry divisions were being reactivated. Therefore, infantry second lieutenants were in great demand, and I expected to be called soon. Things did not work out that way.

The Army notified me that although I was going to receive a regular Army commission, it could not be granted until I turned twenty-one on August 17. However, if I came on active duty from the U.S. Army Reserve immediately, I would be converted to regular Army status after my twenty-first birthday. I decided to wait. I do not know if my decision was based on my lack of trust that this would happen, or if there was some reluctance to go to Korea earlier than necessary. It was probably some of both. That choice had a significant effect on where I spent my first few years of service.

My twenty-first birthday passed with no word from the Army. Ginia and I were staying at my parent's home on the farm and working in Cordele. She worked in the clerical department of Roobin's, and I sold clothing at B.C. Moore's across the street.

In September, I was ordered to Fort McPherson in Atlanta for a pre-commissioning physical examination. A few weeks later, orders came for me to take the commissioning oath on October 3. I did this before a local probate judge with my proud father in attendance. Yet, I still had not received orders to active duty.

Written orders finally arrived the last week in October. I remember the discussion I had with Ginia and my dad.

"They told me to report to the Fourth Infantry Division at Fort Benning by November tenth," I began, "and there is no mention of the Infantry Officer's Basic Course or going to Korea."

"Maybe the division is getting ready to go to Korea," Ginia suggested. "I'm just glad you don't have to go to Korea yet."

I was anxious for more details but did not know who to contact.

My father said, "Fort Benning is only eighty miles away. Why not go there and see what you can learn?"

I did exactly that on November 6. I found the 4th Infantry Division headquarters and asked the sergeant in the front of the room, "Where can I get some information about the division?"

He asked curtly, "Have you signed in yet?"

"No," I answered.

He pointed to a book by the door. "Sign in over there."

I signed in but that proved to be a mistake on my part.

Our wedding on August 7, 1949.

ROTC ball at the University of Georgia, 1950.

CHAPTER 6
Fort Benning: 1950–1951

"You are now officially signed in for duty," the sergeant stated. Without realizing it, I was now "on duty." I was given directions to my unit—Company A, 1st Battalion, 22nd Infantry Regiment, located in the Harmony Church area. I did not have a razor, toothbrush, or spare clothing.

Like a good soldier, I headed for Harmony Church in mid-afternoon. The regimental headquarters was located in the same cantonment area I was in during ROTC camp the previous summer. I reported to the regimental commander, Colonel Lewis B. Riggins—a man in his fifties with a generous stomach. He welcomed me, said a few words about the regiment and then dwelled on the need to buy a trench coat for use in cold or rainy weather. I knew right away that I was not joining one of the Army's top-notch outfits.

The 4th Infantry Division was being activated and trained to become part of NATO, the North Atlantic Treaty Organization, which had been formed to defend against possible Soviet aggression in Europe. Following the Soviet buildup in Eastern Europe, there was concern that the Cold War might turn into a "hot" war. Plans were for the division to obtain, equip, and train a full complement of personnel and move to Germany in the spring 1951.

I contacted Ginia and gave her the news.

She was dismayed. "I don't understand. You don't have to report until the tenth! Why can't you go back then?"

I was hard-pressed to give her a reasonable answer. "Ginia, that is just the way it is; I made a mistake by signing in and I am in too far now to change things. Everything will be fine. Just ask my dad to bring you over here tonight with a few of my personal things and a change of clothes."

She agreed and added, "When can I join you?"

"Just as soon as I can find a place for us to stay. Right now I am in the bachelor officers' quarters."

My father drove her to Fort Benning that night with the things I needed, and she picked up our car. She needed it more than I did.

My new unit had a long and illustrious past. The 1st Battalion of the 22nd Infantry Regiment can trace its history back to the Civil War in 1861. It became part of the 22nd Infantry when the regiment was designated in 1869. It later fought in the American Indian wars, the Spanish-American War, and World War II. The regimental crest, in the shape of a shield, symbolizes the wars the regiment participated in.

In spite of its past achievements, my impression of the unit and army life was not good. The bachelor officers' quarters (BOQ) was the same kind of wooden two-story barracks structure I lived in as an ROTC student—forty officers with cots, foot lockers, and a common latrine. The dining facility was my company's mess hall.

The enlisted ranks also reflected the Army's lack of depth in personnel. There were a few senior regular Army NCOs, but most of the other NCOs were called back from civilian life to help fill the division's ranks. All of our other enlisted troops were right out of basic training. We were a long way from being a combat-ready unit.

My company commander was an army reserve captain in his midforties. He was overweight, out of shape, and did not want to be there. Shortly after I arrived, he became sick and was hospitalized with pneumonia. He never returned. We had no first lieutenants and only three second lieutenants. I was senior to the others by three days date of rank, and I became acting company commander.

I was not prepared for the responsibility but had sense enough to listen to First Sergeant Walter Ginn and a few other key NCOs. Somehow, we managed to keep things going for about six weeks until regular Army First Lieutenant Charles E. Garwood was assigned as company commander. He was a sharp, physically fit, energetic leader and was just what I expected in a professional. He was my first mentor and a good one. His wife, Candy, introduced Ginia to the role of an army wife.

Ginia joined me in late November. We were to be at Fort Benning for only six months and money was short. My salary of $225 plus $42 in food allowance and $65 in quarters allowance barely allowed us to rent the necessary furniture: mattress, sofa, chest of drawers, card table, and two folding chairs. Ginia wanted to work and found a clerical job at Kirven's department store in Columbus. I could not object. We needed the money, and she was getting bored having nothing to do.

My unit worked long, hard hours getting ready for deployment. We had to accomplish advanced individual training for the new men and unit training at platoon and company levels. We also participated in field exercises involving the rest of the battalion but none involving the regiment. Our company spent a lot of time in the field—often a week at a time. I still remember a very cold week we spent on a rifle range where almost everything froze. I did not know it could be so cold in Georgia.

On most days, Ginia drove me to work by 5 a.m. and picked me up whenever we finished training, sometimes late at night. Because I did much of the instruction for my platoon, I had to prepare for the next day's training after getting home at night. In those days, the Army also worked until noon every Saturday. We used every minute we had to bring the unit up to speed, and there was little opportunity for a home life. There were times when I began to have misgivings about my decision to become an army officer.

Somehow we found time to socialize with fellow officers and their wives. First Lieutenant Garwood and his wife invited all Company A officers and their wives to dinner shortly after arrival. That is where Ginia became known as Ginny.

I introduced her. "Sir, this is my wife Ginia."

"Nice to meet you, Ginny!" he replied. Neither she nor I wanted to correct him so the new name stuck.

We became very close to the Garwoods. Chuck was a superb mentor and I learned much from his tutelage. Ginny and I stayed in touch with Chuck and his wife after retirement. He has since passed away as have all those who mentored me as a young officer.

We also found time for Ginny to become pregnant. She had a tough time with morning sickness which often lasted all day. She survived on saltine crackers and ginger ale. Unfortunately, I was not available to help her very much. Yet she never complained; she was a good soldier.

Preparations for our unit to depart for Germany were complete in May 1951, and we started the movement of troops and equipment to seaports. I was then the executive officer of Company A. Master Sergeant Allen, my former platoon sergeant, and I were designated to be on the advance party for the 1st Battalion. First Lieutenant Glenn D. Belnap, another sharp, regular Army officer, was assigned as assistant operations officer of the battalion and headed our group. Our job was to precede the regimental main body and make sure everything was prepared for the arrival of our respective units.

We boarded a troop train headed to Fort Dix, New Jersey, for subsequent movement to a port in New York City. My parents and Ginny saw me off, and parting was extremely difficult. I parked the car near the boarding area and we said our goodbyes.

Mother reminded us, "Three years will pass before we are reunited. They will be long years."

Dad added, "Who knows what will happen in that length of time? Maybe we can find a way to visit you in Germany."

I agreed and assured them, "I will be fine and will write often."

Ginny walked away with me a short distance. I stopped and turned her toward me. Her eyes were watering and I could feel tears start to roll down my cheeks. My heart ached and I said, "Leaving you is the hardest thing I have ever faced. I love you so very much and I will miss you terribly."

She responded, "I have dreaded this day. I know I need to be strong but I can't."

"I know, it is the same with me," I replied, hugging her tightly. "But you are the one with the biggest burden. I am supposedly going on an adventure. You have to stay here, live with your parents, have our baby, and handle things by yourself until you can join me. I wish it could be different."

"Promise to write often?"

"Every day!" I replied. "We will get through this and be together again." I gave her a kiss that would have to last for a long time and then turned toward the train and life without her loving presence.

The new second lieutenant, 1950.

*Ready to depart for Germany with
First Lieutenant Glenn D. Belnap, 1951.*

CHAPTER 7
Troop Duty In Germany, 1951–1954

We arrived at Fort Dix late the following day. My friend, Glenn Belnap, suggested we go to New York to see the sights. This was my first time in a big city and it was a memorable evening. We saw *The Rockettes*, the Broadway play *Gentlemen Prefer Blondes*, and also visited a few night-clubs.

After a five-day trip across the Atlantic aboard the troop transport USNS General Patch, we arrived at the port of Bremerhaven, Germany en route to a supply depot in Mannheim, Germany. This was the staging area for the 4th Infantry Division where troops, equipment, and supplies consolidated for further movement to assigned unit areas in West Germany.

Glenn was a professional officer. Short like me, he was pleasant looking with dark hair. He was intelligent, had high standards, and demonstrated good judgment. I valued his friendship and his advice.

But there was one occasion where he led me astray. After getting our battalion headquarters and the five company areas set up, we had some free time before the units arrived. Glenn and I used the time to get acquainted with the German culture and people in Mannheim. We had a few beers, and I woke up the next morning with a horrible headache.

I asked a member of a local troop unit, "What hit me?"

He responded, "German beer. It has a much higher alcohol content than American beer."

Shortly after the regiment assembled, we relocated to our assigned area inside the town of Schweinfurt. Unlike the United States where land was plentiful, land was scarce in Germany. Army units were stationed in towns and limited to very little local training space. Training above squad-level and all live firing had to be conducted at the few large training areas available elsewhere and on a scheduled basis. Necessarily, we followed suit. This would add to the time spent in the field away from family.

The town of Schweinfurt had a large ball-bearing factory which drew a lot of Allied bombing during World War II. The town still had some debris, as did many of the built-up areas in Germany, but an effort had been made to put things back in order. The German people were work oriented and very organized. They also valued cleanliness. It was common to see the *hausfraus* (housewives) sweeping the streets adjacent to their houses.

A few months after we arrived at Schweinfurt, Glenn was reassigned as executive officer of Company C, and I was moved into his previous job as assistant operations officer of the 1st Battalion. This involved the planning and coordination of training and field operations for the battalion. It gave me the opportunity to learn staff work.

We had come a long way from those early days at Fort Benning. We were professionals and competing with other units for regimental and division honors in numerous activities. My new job kept me very busy and helped me cope with being away from Ginny.

Family quarters were in short supply in the Schweinfurt area and consisted of just a few houses requisitioned from their German owners as war reparations. A permanent army family housing area was under construction but would not be ready for a while. Ginny and I decided to do as many others had done. She and our child would come to Germany as U.S. citizens at our expense and find local housing until army quarters became available. Once in the country, she would at least be eligible for army benefits such as medical care and use of the commissary and the post exchange.

On August 26, 1951, I received a telegram. It was a short but sweet message provided through the services of the Red Cross. "Your wife has given birth to a six pound boy named Wade. Both are fine."

Ginny and I had discussed names and decided to use Wade after my father if she had a boy.

I was elated and went from room to room in the BOQ yelling, "I have a son! I have a son!"

Glenn said, "This calls for a celebration!"

I replied, "Dinner is on me." While at dinner, I bought cigars for everyone.

My normal way of communicating with Ginny was by letter. Trans-atlantic telephone service at that time was undependable, difficult, and expensive, so we used it infrequently. However, Wade's birth justified a call to Vienna.

I told Ginny, "Thank you for giving me a son! I am so happy and yet so sorry not to have been there to help you through the process. Just know that I am grateful."

Meanwhile, Colonel Riggins, still the regimental commander, decided we needed a full-time school to train new NCOs and improve the skills of selected NCOs. Glenn was chosen to run the school and he chose me to help him. We set up the school in one of the unused airfield hangars, found some equipment, and selected a few smart NCOs to help with the instruction. We started the 22nd Infantry NCO Academy and had a great time. We were on our own and could see the results of our work when students graduated each month.

In addition, we were not affected by the frequent readiness alerts conducted by and for the regiment. We were exempt so our normal school schedule was not interrupted. These alerts were initiated without prior notice, mostly at night or on weekends. The regiment would be given an order to assemble and move to its defensive areas some distance away and be prepared to fight. This had to be completed in a matter of hours, and the operation was watched very closely. Failure to accomplish this in a timely manner brought serious consequences for the commander of the unit concerned.

Not having after-hour responsibilities, Glenn and I had more leisure time. This could have been a time of temptation for us. There were more German women than German men due to their wartime losses. Therefore U.S. soldiers, particularly officers, were in great demand. Some of my married brothers-in-arms whose wives had not yet arrived soon found German female companions and set up housekeeping with them off post. This was frowned upon, especially by the wives already in the country, and was considered conduct unbecoming to an officer—a violation of army regulations. But no one was reprimanded, unless something worse happened because of the affair. There were consequences—many relationships led to divorce.

Glenn and I enjoyed our leisure time. He bought a small German car. (Most European cars were small.) On weekends, we explored the countryside, venturing as far as Frankfurt and Munich—both within a day's drive. We tried German cuisine and found it delicious and inexpensive due to the monetary exchange rate.

Schnitzel and sauerbraten were my favorites. Schnitzel is thin slices of pork fried in a tasty batter. Sauerbraten is beef slices soaked in a mild vinegar sauce, broiled, then rolled up and wrapped with a dill pickle. One could exchange a single U.S. dollar for four deutsche marks and have a great steak dinner with a green salad and fried potatoes.

Wade was six months old when I first saw him. Ginny wrote almost daily and she sent me a few photos of her holding him. She would write a few details.

"Wade is really focusing on things around him now."

"He is not taking to my milk and we are trying different substitutes."

"I am telling him about his father."

Although these notes helped me, it was not the same as being with him or holding him.

However, the day finally came in February 1952, when Ginny and Wade arrived at the port of Bremerhaven. (My father thought it was dangerous for them to fly overseas so he arranged for them to go by ship.) She and Wade traveled on the USS *United States,* a civilian passenger ship, along with many other army wives. Fortunately, Ginny had a cabin mate who helped with Wade when Ginny got seasick during some rough weather.

Meeting them when the ship arrived was a wonderful moment. I had missed her terribly and longed to hold Wade. The snow was falling as I boarded the ship and located Ginny's cabin. I saw her standing by the door of their cabin with Wade in her arms.

Finally. I sighed and put my arms around both of them.

Neither of us said anything for a moment. We just basked in the feeling of our closeness. Then she said to me, "Meet your son."

We parted. I looked down at Wade. "Can I hold him?"

She laughed. "It is time you learned how."

I took him from her and held my precious little boy. "Let us get acquainted."

A few hours later we boarded a night train back to Schweinfurt. Unbelievably, Ginny, Wade, and I stayed together in a single, upper bunk of a railway car that night. She and I talked most of the night.

Initially, we lived in a *gasthaus* (pension) until we could get our own quarters. This was a room over a bar and restaurant located in a nearby village. Glenn loaned me his car to go back and forth to work. It snowed heavily for the first few days and traveling back and forth was tough. But I didn't mind. Ginny and I had a second honeymoon and I got to know my son. He was a joy to hold and I was awed by his small and perfect features. He was a healthy, chubby, smiling, blue-eyed little boy.

I was finally assigned family quarters in the town of Schweinfurt—a small duplex located in residential Schweinfurt, complete with a live-in housekeeper. Marcelle was a middle-aged French woman, the widow of a German soldier. It was a pleasure to have such an unexpected benefit. In addition to keeping the house clean, she took care of Wade. She became like family and we corresponded for years afterward.

We could not get too comfortable. There was always the threat of a Soviet attack and the use of atomic weapons. If "the balloon went up" as we referred to an attack with atomic weapons, I would go with my unit to our defensive positions. Ginny and Wade would board an army bus and evacuate to an assembly area near Frankfurt and await air evacuation out of the country. Ginny kept an emergency bag packed at all times.

Our reunion was short-lived. As more U.S. Army divisions joined NATO, a realignment of defensive responsibilities was necessary. In the process, a newly-arrived unit moved into Schweinfurt and our regiment had to relocate. Although the regiment moved to Geissen, the NCO Academy was moved elsewhere—to Wildflecken, a former remote German Army training area located about seventy-five miles from Schweinfurt. This provided a better environment for our training and kept us away from the normal distractions of being in close proximity to the regiment.

Wildflecken (meaning wild spot) did not have any family quarters. My family and Glenn's family remained in Schweinfurt. We were the only officers with the academy, so we took turns going to Schweinfurt via train on weekends. This situation lasted a few months, until the division commander visited. When he learned where our families were, he located quarters for us in Bad Kissingen, a resort town about halfway between Schweinfurt and Wildflecken. Both of our families were moved there. The houses were nice, the town was beautiful, and the travel time was much shorter. Marcelle came with us, and we started paying her full salary.

Just as Ginny and I were becoming comfortable with our family life, the situation changed again. A large German house became available in Giessen for the NCO Academy, so we relocated the academy. Then Glenn and I both left the school. He was made commander of the regimental headquarters company. I became the assistant operations and training officer for the 22nd Infantry.

I enjoyed my new job. On field exercises, I went to the division headquarters, kept them abreast of what my regiment was doing, and provided a liaison between the two headquarters. In garrison, I helped to plan and coordinate training for the regiment. Trips to see Ginny and Wade were infrequent. Ginny and Glenn's wife, Jean, became close friends and helped each other in times of need.

My job changed again. I was reassigned to a troop unit, the best place for an infantry officer. I became the executive officer of Company G, 2nd Battalion, 22nd Infantry. At that time the entire regiment was located in permanent facilities just outside the town of Kirschgoins.

Meanwhile family quarters twelve miles away at Bad Nauheim became available, and many families were reunited, including mine. Our apartment was nice but on the fourth floor. (The criterion for quarters' assignment seemed to be the lower one's rank, the higher the apartment.)

We were so happy to be together that its location did not bother us, except when there were groceries to bring home. Marcelle came with Ginny and lived in the maid's quarters in the basement. Everything was convenient. There was a lovely park across the street with a lake and ducks for Wade to watch. His personality was developing quickly, and I enjoyed playing with him in the evenings. The post exchange and commissary were also within walking distance. All the regiment's families lived in the same area and socialized actively. Life was good whenever the regiment was not in the field. Life was so good that Ginny became pregnant again.

Although I worked long hours and was often away at major training areas or on maneuvers, Ginny and I still found time for some short vacations. We took a long weekend trip to Paris.

We went to see *Les Folies Bergere* one night. I ended up sitting directly behind a post.

Ginny laughed and said, "That is the perfect seat for you!"

I could not enjoy the half-clothed females singing and dancing because I couldn't see them. Ginny was perfectly content with that.

We spent another weekend in Garmisch near the Alps. The U.S. Army used that area as a recreational center. It was a beautiful place nestled at the foot of the mountains. Hitler's mountaintop retreat (Hitler's Nest) was at nearby Berchtesgaden and we found it very interesting. (The recreational center is still there today.)

My three-year overseas tour would be completed in May 1954, and I would rotate back to a stateside assignment. We had to make a decision regarding our future. My four-year active duty service commitment finished in November 1954 and that would affect my upcoming reassignment. Ginny and I had talked about this. I reviewed our experiences.

"We have spent lots of time apart so far. This could be the norm."

She countered, "But we have had great times when we have been together. I have enjoyed the feeling of being part of the regimental family."

I reminded her, "We have not seen our families or had the advantages of living in the United States for quite a while."

She responded, "But look what we have seen and done!"

"Yes," I said. "That has been interesting. I'm proud to be a soldier and wear the Infantry's insignia. I am serving my country and enjoying it. I have four years of service and can retire in six more if I choose."

She quipped, "A nice choice to have."

Following our discussion, I submitted an assignment preference form, indicating a desire for further active service, preferably troop duty at Fort Benning.

The Department of the Army responded with orders to the 47th Infantry Division at Fort Benning with temporary duty en route to attend a three-month course at Benning. This was a temporary course provided for those who had missed the Infantry Officer's Basic Course (IOBC). I was delighted—we would be close to home and I would still be with troops.

This time we traveled together. From Frankfurt, we flew Trans World Airlines in a propeller-powered plane with a group of army families headed for New York. It was a long, miserable trip with stops in Shannon, Ireland; the Azores; and Newfoundland. Ginny was six months pregnant and uncomfortable.

To make matters worse, Wade had diarrhea and the only toilet was clogged. We finally landed very late that night and were bussed to Fort Hamilton, New York, where we were given a room with cots and blankets. We then learned that we were quarantined there for several weeks. Two of the children sitting directly behind us had chickenpox. Their faces had been powdered to disguise the disease, but it was detected when they were processed through customs and immigration. Ginny already had chickenpox as a child, and it was now too late to worry about Wade or me getting it. We crashed that night.

The next morning, the quarantine had been lifted. We never knew why but were happy to get out of there and catch a flight to Atlanta where my parents met us.

Thirty days leave of absence had been authorized between duty stations. This was intended to be a nice vacation but did not turn out that way. After a week, I began to develop flu-like symptoms and a doctor came to examine me. (Doctors still made house calls then!) He thought I might be developing pneumonia. However, the next morning I had chicken pox all over my body—even in my hair. The rest of my leave was spent enduring a classic case of the pox. Wade got it next.

Ginny joins me in Germany, 1952.

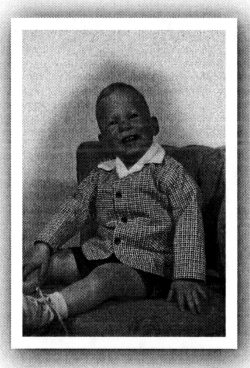

Wade Shannon Steele at age two.

First lieutenant in Germany, 1954.

CHAPTER 8
Troop and Instructor
Duty at Benning: 1954–1958

By the time my leave was up, I was well enough to go to Fort Benning. We were given a two-bedroom apartment. We parlayed our $500 savings into a 1954 Chevy and enough furniture to get by with. We were happy but in debt.

I was attending my infantry school course when Ginny went into labor. She had often joked, "I will try and have the baby on your birthday."

When my class returned from a field exercise the afternoon of my birthday, the first sergeant of the company to which we were assigned told me, "You got a call this afternoon. Your wife has gone into the hospital to have her baby."

I rushed over to the hospital. The nurse said, "Your wife is getting ready to go into the delivery room."

I sat in the lobby to wait and started studying for a test. Before long, I saw a stretcher coming down the long hallway. As it got closer, I saw Ginny on it and went to meet her. "Honey, are you going to the delivery room now?"

"No, I've already been! Your new son is right here with me."

I looked and there he was lying quietly right between her legs. I sputtered, "But the nurse told me you were waiting to go!"

I was embarrassed, proud, and happy at the same time. Had I not made an A on the test the following day, she might have given me some slack. However, she told this story many times.

We had not settled on a name. "Let's name him Richard. That is a good English name," I suggested.

"No, how about Rodney?"

"I don't like that one. It sounds sissy."

And so it went on and on. We just could not come up with a good choice. The nurse finally said, "You must name him today. We have to record his birth."

Ginny answered, "He was born on my husband's birthday so we will name the baby for his father—William Berry Steele Junior."

★★★

Following my schooling, I joined the 47th Infantry Division, a National Guard unit called to active duty to train and be available for deployment. This division would reinforce the U.S. forces located in West Germany in the event of a Soviet military attack. I was assigned as executive officer of an infantry rifle company commanded by Captain Marion L. Chalker. We worked well together until he departed to attend the Infantry Officer's Advanced Course (IOAC). This was a nine-month course designed to prepare officers for command and staff duty at battalion and brigade levels. I became the acting commander until a captain became available.

I soon met Captain Wally Veaudry who commanded another company in the same battalion. We became friends, and he was a good mentor. He saw intense combat action with one of the first infantry units rushed from Hawaii to Korea in 1950. He and I served together several times, and our families were close for many years.

In 1956, the Army experimented with different combat organizations to determine the effectiveness of these organizations in a nuclear war environment. The 47th Infantry Division was reorganized and redesignated the 3rd Infantry Division. My company became Company E, 30th Infantry Brigade Combat Team, under the command of Captain Albert E. Rosner.

A paratrooper who had served in an airborne division, Captain Rosner was sharp, tough, and highly motivated. He quickly set out to imbue our company with the same morale and esprit as the airborne unit in which he had served.

He showed me how little things challenged people to meet higher standards. He said, "Everyone likes to be a winner and special. We just have to give them pride and motivation in what they are doing."

He set high standards, created a unit nickname, instituted tough morning runs, introduced a marching chant, and provided tee shirts with our unit name and emblem. Our company soon stood out among other rifle companies. Unfortunately, after a few months, he left to attend school. I took over the company again.

The division engaged in the largest maneuver since World War II: Operation Sagebrush. Its purpose was to test the new nuclear war-fighting concepts for which we had trained. It lasted six weeks, involved several divisions, and maneuvered over the states of Alabama, Mississippi, and Louisiana. I learned a lot about tactics, rapid movement, and the increased challenges in communications and logistics.

I was promoted to captain on April 6, 1956, and went to the regimental headquarters as the assistant operations and training officer. We spent much time in the field on regimental command post exercises (CPX). (These were map exercises without troops.) This enabled me to learn a lot about planning and monitoring the tactical movement of troop units.

The regimental operations sergeant, Master Sergeant Mike Dunn, was a tough individual from the old school and addressed me in third person. He had a lot of staff experience, and he taught "the captain" much about producing good operation orders and running an efficient operations shop. Mike kept in contact with me until he passed away in the late 1990s. (I usually received one or two calls from him yearly—usually late at night—with indications that he had consumed a few adult beverages.) I think he took pride in each of my promotions.

During this tour of duty, we took advantage of holidays to visit relatives since we missed out on family activities while we were overseas. We wanted Wade and Billy to get to know their Akin cousins: James Reuben and Shannon Akin; Bob and Doug Gill (and later a sister, Beth); Roddy and Rita Attaway; and Allen Akin. The children had great fun playing in the big house on Union Street in Vienna, and the adults had a good time talking. We stayed up late at night. Woe to the ones who went to bed early, for they were talked about in their absence.

By this time I was well grounded in company-level responsibilities and was selected to attend the IOAC at Fort Benning. Because we would remain at Benning at least another year, we decided to upgrade our accommodations and our lifestyle. Ginny wanted to work again, too.

One morning, she remarked, "You are leaving me without a car and taking the last pack of cigarettes with you!"

Her point was certainly correct. But that was not all she wished for.

"We need more living space, and I want to get into a house and have more privacy."

Although agreeing with her, I countered, "Sounds good but how can we afford it? Who will take care of the boys?"

Ginny replied, "I can get a job. I can get someone to clean house and care for the children until I get home in mid-afternoon."

Ginny applied for a teaching position in the Fort Benning school system and was accepted to teach fourth grade. With her working, we could afford a house near the post. Wade was in the first grade, and we found a woman to stay with the children until Ginny arrived home from school.

Around 200 officers were in my class, many of whom had served in

Korea. Some had distinguished themselves in combat. (I had not even heard a shot fired in anger.) Many of us became close friends and served together over the years. During classroom work, we were seated alphabetically and one of my seatmates was Captain Joe Starker. We soon became best friends and later served together on several occasions.

The IOAC was great and provided me with the foundation to solve problems in every subsequent assignment. Many of us served together again and knew each other's strengths. We worked hard, but we also played hard, visiting with friends or attending class parties.

After five years in troop command and staff jobs, I was ready for an instructor assignment. I requested to teach at the Infantry School at Fort Benning, and Joe Starker asked for the same. He and I also requested the Basic Airborne Course and the Jumpmaster Course en route. The former was training to become a parachutist while the latter provided leaders with the skills needed to lead in the combat parachuting process. The two courses lasted a total of five weeks.

At the same time, we submitted applications to attend flight training. The Army had just gained operational control of fixed-wing propeller aircraft and helicopters. More pilots were needed. Pilots received extra pay and were getting in on the ground floor of something new. Joe was accepted. I was turned down because of difficulty in hearing high frequency sounds. I was disappointed, but it was probably for the best. I was not very coordinated.

My assignment as an instructor with the Infantry School with airborne and jumpmaster schooling en route cheered me up. This meant another two or three years at Benning. We were overjoyed—so were our families.

When my IOAC ended, I was designated "Distinguished Graduate" for my class. This served to offset my earlier feelings of inadequacies felt around my combat-decorated peers. It also helped me receive early promotion to the rank of major.

In August 1957, I went directly to the Basic Airborne Course. The weather was unusually hot and our training was outside and very physical. We were wet with sweat most of the day and I was very tired at night. There were boots and brass to shine in order to pass the next morning's inspection. Failure to pass inspection meant many extra pushups. The training was great and each jump was thrilling. After graduation and a week's respite, I reported for my job at the Infantry School.

In addition to several of my classmates who stayed as instructors, some of my earlier friends were also there: Captain Chuck Garwood and Captain Glenn Belnap from the 4th Division, plus Captain Wally Veaudry from the 3rd Division. Wherever I went, I found old friends. The school was a great assignment.

I was given responsibility for the curriculum of several courses, including the Basic Airborne Course. The latter responsibility carried with it a "jump slot." Therefore, I made one or more jumps each month for an additional $110 per month.

I had my evenings and weekends free to play with Wade and Billy. They were both very active and healthy. Wade was slightly chubby and his hair was now sandy-colored. Billy was growing fast but was slim and had dark hair. We had a yard to enjoy and time to use it. We went to movies in town and enjoyed the drive-in theaters, often stopping for hot dogs or hamburgers on the way. On Sunday afternoons, we rode around Columbus and made a routine stop at Kinnett's Dairy for ice cream. We all looked forward to that, especially the boys. In late December 1958, my ideal assignment ended.

Rifle Company Commander at Fort Benning, 1955.

Ginny, Wade, and Billy at our Fort Benning apartment, 1956.

Distinguished Graduate for the 1957 Class of the
IOAC at the U.S. Army Infantry School.

Home of the Akin family in Vienna, Georgia, from 1935–1964.

CHAPTER 9

Advisory Role in Saudi Arabia: 1959

Orders came for me to go to a six-week course on the Middle East, followed by assignment as military advisor to the Royal Guard Regiment in Saudi Arabia.

I was surprised and told Ginny, "I didn't realize that we had people in Saudi Arabia."

"You were expecting assignment to Korea, weren't you?"

"Yes. I was due for an unaccompanied tour and figured it would be a twelve-month assignment to Korea without you and the kids."

She consoled me. "Well you will have an opportunity to see some of the Middle East."

"I suppose so," I remarked. "But I would have preferred to be with an American unit."

In early January 1958, I went to Washington, D.C. to attend a U.S. Department of State course on Middle Eastern culture and the history of Saudi Arabia. As an infantry officer, I was not accustomed to such first-class treatment—a nice apartment, classrooms in a civilian facility, and a per-diem allowance for food.

Following the course, I said a sad farewell to my family. "Goodbyes do not get any easier," I told Ginny.

"No," she said. "But we knew this was coming."

"You will be the one with the heavy load again. You will have the boys to care for, teach school, and handle all the household chores I used to help you with."

"Don't worry, Bill. Just take care of yourself." She sighed. "We will get through this and be together again."

The year spent in Saudi Arabia was not very productive. The U.S. Military Training Mission (USMTM) could only advise because the Saudi government paid for the equipment they received from the United States. Thus, we had no leverage to encourage them to follow our advice.

The mission included representatives from other services and departments. I was part of a small group of six (three officers and three NCOs) advising the king's Royal Guard Regiment. The Royal Guard was adjacent to King Saud's Palace in the capital city of Riyadh.

The palace walls and all the buildings were painted bright pink. I had a chance to see the palace rooms in which ceremonies took place, but the rest was off limits to us. The rooms were beautifully decorated in vivid greens, reds, and gold. The furniture was ornate and trimmed in gold. Doorways and mantels carried intricate designs and Oriental rugs were in abundance. It was an impressive sight reminding me of European palaces.

Our group of six lived in a house owned by the prince of the Royal Guard near the palace. We went to the mission house for our meals, to play volleyball, or see a rooftop movie at night. Non-Islamic religious services were not allowed. Yet, on occasion, an air force chaplain dressed in civilian clothing flew in on the embassy "milk run," and while the plane was refueling, we had a short service behind a locked door.

My job was to advise Colonel Abdullah Suleiman, the 1st Battalion commander, and we became good friends, in spite of our language difficulties. However, I never felt comfortable with him holding my hand while we were walking. In that culture, this was a display of trust and friendship.

The soldiers were from desert tribes and had little knowledge of mechanical things. However, they were eager to learn and quick to show their appreciation. Our unit's primary mission was protection of the large royal family. Tactical training was minimal and field training was limited. I received an Army Commendation Medal for meritorious service in Saudi Arabia. But, if I had any real impact, it was during the thirty days of Ramadan, a religious holiday. I taught leadership and map reading to four colonels of the regiment. During that time, I talked about life in the United States and tried to give them a feel for democracy.

Because of the heat, the regiment worked only during the morning hours. Thus we had a lot of free time. Unfortunately, there was not much to do for entertainment. Life was very austere in Arabia: no alcohol, no movies, no television, no sports, and no smoking. If anyone was seen smoking a cigarette in public, it was struck from his hand by one of the religious police wielding a stick.

I took advantage of the free time to make several short trips on the shuttle flight between embassy activities. These trips included Jedah and Dhahran in Saudi Arabia and Asmara in Ethiopia. Our medical support was at the U.S. Air Force Base in Dhahran. We were always happy to go there and hit the bar—where milkshakes were served. It was also on the coast of the Gulf of Arabia and offered swimming—if swimming with large jelly fish was not bothersome.

A trip to Dhahran had a bonus feature. One could call home via a radio/telephone connection. The few times I went there, I called Ginny. A phone calle was worth more than a stack of letters. Just hearing her voice gave me much happiness. She had a busier life than I did. I remember feeling guilty on numerous occasions.

"I just came down from getting Wade's kite off the roof."

Another time she said, "I had to take Billy to the emergency room today. He tried to put a dog into a sewer and it bit him on the lip."

The highlight of my tour was a week of leave -time spent visiting the Holy Land. I flew into Jerusalem and joined a tour that went to many of the biblical sights in the area: Bethlehem, Bethany, The Jordan River, and the Dead Sea. We floated easily in the brackish water, but it wasn't pleasant . The water was dark brown—almost black—extremely heavy, and very salty. Even the beach was unpleasant—large grains of dark sand with an occasional pebble. I did not stay in long and wanted a bath afterwards.

Because my tour ended in early January, the Army generously brought me back to the States just before Christmas 1958. This was nice Christmas present for me and my family.

Captain and advisor to the King's Royal Guard Regiment, Saudi Arabia, 1958.

Ginny while teaching school in Columbus, 1958.

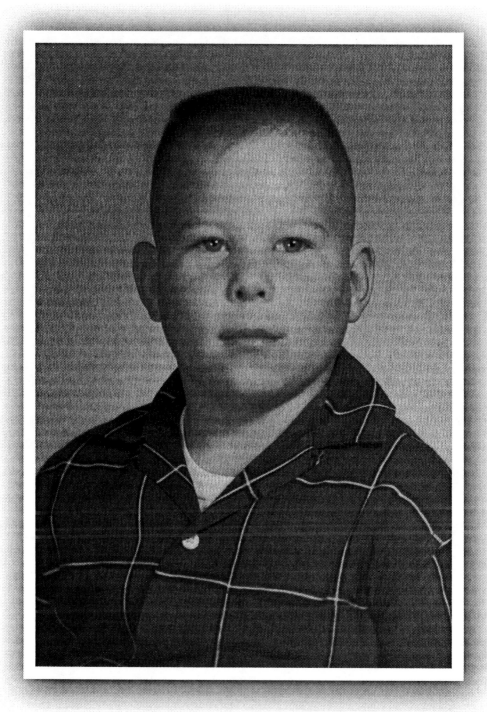

Wade Steele, 1958.

CHAPTER 10

Airborne Duty And Navy College: 1960–1963

After the advisory duty in Saudi Arabia, my next assignment request was for more troop duty, specifically with an airborne unit. Again, my request was honored. I was assigned to the 82nd Airborne Division at Fort Bragg, North Carolina, with thirty days leave en route.

The Air Force flew me from Dhahran to Shaw Air Force Base near Charleston, South Carolina. From there I took a bus to Columbus. Ginny met me at 2 a.m.

After one long kiss she moved her head back and said, "The mustache has to go!"

We stayed awake talking until the boys woke up, and we all had a big reunion.

During the holidays, we caught up on visits with relatives and readjusted to living together again. Ginny had been independent for a year. She was accustomed to handling our finances, and I was happy for her to continue. However, use of the car was different. After some persuasion, she finally agreed to let me share the car with her.

In early January 1960, we loaded the car and headed for Fort Bragg. The car was almost new; we had traded in the 1954 green Plymouth four-door sedan for a used, sporty, white 1958 Buick two-door hardtop. Our quarters were on post—a three-bedroom apartment close to the 82nd Airborne Division area. In addition, the boy's school was within walking distance.

The U.S. Army was stationed around the world because there were so many potential trouble spots. Our strategy called for a rapid response force—a force that could be moved quickly to reinforce our troops in some location or to block aggression until other forces had time to get there. The 82nd Airborne Division was that force. It had to be able to move by air to any given location on very short notice. In fact, the first element had to be ready to load within thirty minutes after notification. Obviously, this required a high state-of-combat readiness.

I was proud to be a part of the division and looked forward to the challenge. It was operating under a new organizational concept that called for a division to have five small battle groups rather than three larger regiments. Because of its priority, the division was kept at full strength in men and equipment. This was a luxury to me because that had not been the case in my previous troop assignments. I was sent to the 503rd Airborne Battle Group, commanded by Colonel Gus Peters. He was a big, stocky, former West Point football player, who still looked the part. He gave me command of Company E.

Company E was well trained and First Sergeant Carl Griffin was professional. I named us Echo's Eagles and had tee shirts designed for use on our morning runs through the division area. (Echo is the army phonetic for the letter E.) A few other Rosner techniques set us apart from other companies. When we passed the dreaded annual inspection with the rating of "Best Company in the Division," we were really set apart. The icing on the cake, however, was winning a three-day field exercise against units of the 101st Airborne Division at Camp Mackall later that year. Not everything was perfect, though. Weapons security was mandatory and anyone losing a weapon paid for it. Two pistols were stolen from my company arms room and I had to pay for them.

During the exercise against the 101st Airborne Division, our operations officer was seriously injured in a helicopter accident and taken to a naval hospital in Virginia for treatment. I and three other captains went by helicopter to visit him. As we were landing, the pilot told me he had radioed ahead and informed the airfield control tower that he was inbound with four captains who were going to visit the hospital. When we landed, I was surprised that a navy commander and two navy sedans were there to greet us. But when I saw the look on the navy commander's face, I realized someone had thought we were navy captains—the equivalent of an army colonel. I told him one sedan was sufficient.

Aside from normal training and garrison activities, we spent a lot of time on individual readiness for combat. We had to be up-to-date on vaccinations against diseases anywhere in the world, our wills had to be current, our weapons qualifications had to be maintained, and everyone had to have a monthly training jump. (While there I qualified for the Senior Parachutist Badge.)

One battle group had to be on a twenty-four-hour notice (alert) at all times, and the duty was rotated weekly. One company of the alert battle group had to be ready to load on aircraft within thirty minutes. These requirements meant that periodically the entire battle group had to be on a short leash and readily available. Our readiness was tested on several occasions by the division or higher headquarters, and we never knew if it was a test exercise or the real thing. On one occasion, we flew to the Panama Canal Zone and parachuted in at night for a practice drill.

In spite of all this, I loved the duty. The troops were well trained, highly motivated, and tough. They were at their best when they were kept busy. With time on their hands, they could get into trouble. On several Saturday nights, I had to go to Fayetteville and get someone out of the city jail.

After a year in command, I was transferred to the battle group headquarters as S-1 or adjutant. This office handled all personnel matters for the battle group and acted for the commander on administrative matters. This broadened my knowledge of staff work. The battle group S-2 (intelligence officer) was Captain Sam Smithers. Sam and his wife, Tillie, became our close friends. Sam and I served together several more times.

After a few months in that job, I moved to the division staff as an assistant G-1 where I handled officer assignments and other personnel-related actions. The people were professional, friendly, and helpful. The Deputy G-1, Major Gordon Lippmann, was an impressive officer. He started as an enlisted man in the latter part of World War II, won a Distinguished Service Cross, was given a battlefield commission, and had extensive airborne experience. I learned many things from him, including how to work a staff action and present it to the Chief of Staff or one of the general officers and how to network among personnel staffs in higher headquarters. When he moved up to replace the G-1, he recommended me for his old job as Deputy G-1. (Sadly, he was later killed by sniper fire in Vietnam.)

While in this capacity, I and several other officers were designated to be on the staff of a joint command being organized to conduct a joint army, navy, and air force training exercise in the Panama Canal Zone. We were gone for about six weeks. Being on a joint staff was a first for me. I was the J-1 and handled personnel matters for all units of the joint command. Fortunately, only unit headquarters staffs were actually involved, and no troops units were deployed.

While in Panama, I got a copy of the *Army Times,* a newspaper that kept up with army activities and was marketed to army personnel. It contained the list of captains selected for promotion to major. My name was on the list! I did not expect to be considered until the next year when I would be within the time zone for promotion consideration.

I was excited as I explained the news to Ginny. "Each promotion board considers for promotion those officers whose date of rank in their current grade is within a certain time zone. They can recommend a specified number of people for promotion to the grade being considered. But they can pull five percent of their nominees from officers one year below the zone of consideration. I am among the five percent!"

She said, "That's great! You must be doing something right! Did you know you were being considered?"

"No! It was a pleasant surprise."

On return to Fort Bragg, I found that Major Lippmann had been selected to attend the Armed Forces Staff College. I was able to act as G-1 for a few months until we got a lieutenant colonel to fill that slot. I became involved in contingency planning for operations we might conduct in potential trouble spots including Cuba. As it turned out, the Cuban plan we developed was almost put into effect during the Cuban Missile Crisis of 1963.

Fort Bragg was a fine post and family-friendly. We had many friends and neighbors. When our next-door neighbor heard that her husband (Captain Moon assigned to a special forces unit) had been killed in Laos, we knew this was the beginning of our increased military involvement in Southeast Asia and subsequently the Vietnam War.

Ginny taught fifth grade in the post school and we had some quality time together. The boys had many friends to play with and were outside most of the daylight hours.

One Saturday afternoon, a military policeman knocked on the door with two sheepish-looking boys in tow. I looked at him and asked, "What is the matter Corporal?"

"Sir," he said. "These two boys have been throwing rocks into some windows in an old vacant building at the bottom of the hill. They told me they live here."

I looked at Wade, then Billy, and replied, "Yes, they live here and they belong to me. I am sorry this happened. They should have known not to do that and I believe they are sorry they did. Isn't that right boys?"

Wade talked first, "Yes, sir, it was wrong. I am sorry."

Billy followed suit, "I am sorry too."

I spoke up, "Corporal, if you don't take them to jail, I promise to administer their punishment and I don't think they will misbehave again."

"Okay, sir. I will leave them with you."

The boys endured a temporary house arrest.

On another memorable occasion, Wade appeared at the door exclaiming excitedly, "Billy is hurt!"

Ginny ran to Billy. "What happened?"

He replied, "I was riding my wagon down the hill and it hit a tree. Something is wrong with my leg."

Ginny took him to the hospital where he was treated for a broken leg.

★★★

Promotion to the rank of major moved me from company grade to field grade status. (Field grade statuses were major, lieutenant colonel, and full colonel.) When the promotion day came—July 26, 1961—we decided to take advantage and moved to a larger, nicer duplex in the field grade housing area. We were thrilled when we were assigned to live next door to our friends the Smithers. Sam had already been promoted to major. We really enjoyed our relationship and our social life with them. They had two children, Jimmy and Robin, and our two boys played with them often.

In the spring of 1962, selections of officers to attend the next Command and General Staff Course (CGSC) were announced. This was a year-long course at Fort Leavenworth, Kansas, designed to prepare majors and lieutenant colonels of all army branches for command and staff jobs at division, corps, or army level. It was an important course but not everyone could attend.

I made that year's list but was selected to attend the Naval Command and Staff Course (NCSC) at Newport, Rhode Island instead. Each year, a few officers were chosen to attend sister-service schools. It provided some familiarity with the other services and facilitated interservice or joint force operations. It was an honor to be selected, but I missed getting the instruction that my peers received on army matters.

Shortly after the CGSC list came out, the Army formed a board of officers to design plans for developing and testing a new concept for the use of helicopters in a combat role with infantry and armor elements. Lieutenant General Hamilton Howze was named to head it, so it became the Howze Board. It was formed at Fort Bragg, and officers from several installations and units were brought in on temporary duty to work on the board, including me.

This effort defined the concepts for use of army aviation in a combat and combat-support role and led to formation of an air assault division. This concept was tested by the 2nd Infantry Division at Fort Benning. It was then redesignated as the 1st Air Calvary Division and deployed to Vietnam in the early stages of the war. The book and subsequent movie, *We Were Soldiers Once and Young,* were based on the exploits of that unit. It portrayed the first battle that U.S. Army units had with a regular North Vietnamese Army (NVA) unit in November 1965.

While on the Howze Board, I worked with a number of new aviators who went on to fill some important jobs in the Army. Among them was my friend Major Joe Starker. Joe was a key pioneer in Army aviation and one of the first Army aviation general officers. (Joe went on to become a brigadier general but was killed in an automobile accident in his forties.)

In July 1962, Ginny, the boys, and I left Fort Bragg for Newport. With help from the Navy, we located a house near the school that Wade and Billy would attend. It was two blocks from the beach. We had a great time exploring the area and enjoying the seaside atmosphere the week before I was scheduled to start the course. Seafood was in abundance, and we ate a lot of lobster at one dollar a pound.

Ginny was taken aback with her first experience at cooking lobsters. When she tried to pick up a lobster that did not want to be put into a pot of boiling water, she called to Billy.

"Billy, come pick up this lobster for me!"

He replied, "Why can't you do it?"

"It is moving too much."

"It's easy," he said. "Just grab him by the back so he can't claw you."

Billy quickly got the angry lobsters into the pot and that became his exclusive job.

The first week of the navy course was one of orientation for those of us from other services and governmental agencies. That was fun. We spent a day each on a destroyer, aircraft carrier, and submarine which included some under-water time. We also watched the America's Cup Race off the Newport coast from the deck of a navy cruiser.

The Navy knew how to live. The facilities were nice. Like the Air Force, I think the Navy built family facilities before runways or docks in case the money ran out. They also used their Philippine-born cooks in the officer's club. (This may have been why our dues were low.) Seafood buffets were great and cheap.

Our family was happy. The town was small, and the boys could walk downtown to the movie theater, the drug store, the beach, and visit their school friends. Ginny deserved some time to relax. She took a year off from teaching school.

We had one mishap. Billy fell from a low wall in our yard and broke his elbow. He handled it well and endured his cast without much complaint. Somehow he always seemed to find a way to get hurt.

I studied. George Washington University had a graduate degree program integrated with the NCSC. I could get master's degree credit for some of the NCSC work. Completing these and several additional courses taught by the university at night, plus writing a thesis and passing oral exams, qualified me for a master's degree in international relations. The Army paid for my tuition. I decided to take advantage of the opportunity.

The George Washington master's degree program, combined with the NCSC, kept me very busy. Although I was at home more during that nine-month period than at any other time in our married life, most of my time was spent studying and writing over a card table in our bedroom. Without Ginny's help with the typing, I would not have completed the degree program and navy course.

I took some time off over the Christmas holidays. We also enjoyed a weekend trip to explore New England and attended one Boston Red Sox baseball game.

When the NCSC was over, I stayed in Newport for four more weeks to finish the last course and exams for the master's program. We cleared out of the house. Ginny and the boys went to Vienna and I moved into the nearby naval BOQ. I rejoined them for a two-week vacation in Georgia before reporting to my next duty station—Washington D.C.

A major in the 82nd Airborne Division, 1962.

Ginny and the boys at our home in Newport, 1963.

The Akin family celebrating Claude and Oma's wedding anniversary, 1963.
From left to right: R.C., Ginny, Helen, Ruth, Elizabeth, and Johnny.

CHAPTER 11

U.S. Army Staff and War College: 1963–1967

My assignment following the NCSC was to Headquarters, Department of the Army. I worked in the Infantry Officer's Assignment Branch. That small office of about twelve officers handled the assignment and schooling selections for all infantry officers. We were located at Fort McNair in Washington, D.C.

Our friends, the Belnaps, were also in Washington. Glenn was involved in personnel work at the Pentagon. They helped us locate a house near them, and we quickly resumed our friendship. Our house was large, with a basement and lots of space for work and play. Fortunately, it was also within our government housing allowance.

Since the Infantry Officer's Branch determined where all infantry officers were assigned, I felt honored to have been selected to join that group. Initially, my job was to handle the numerous lieutenants. But because of their short time in service, their files were slim and assignments were easy to determine. After a year, I was moved to the school's desk and had responsibility for selecting our candidates for the CGSC as well as those officers we wanted to send to post-graduate civilian schooling. Reviewing voluminous paper files all day and some nights was detailed, tedious work, and I overdosed on coffee and cigarettes. I feel like the

Army Commendation Medal I received for meritorious service during that assignment was well deserved.

This probably contributed to the development of a heart condition known as atrial fibrillation (periodic irregular heartbeat). Although not necessarily debilitating, it could lead to a runaway heartbeat and heart failure. I underwent several tests and was put on medication to regulate the heartbeat. While the medication helped, the irregularity occasionally returned, but usually did not last more than a few hours. Otherwise, I continued to function normally. This gave me the impetus to stop smoking and reduce my coffee intake.

Ginny found a job in the billing office of the Arlington Hospital. She stayed there for about six months until she got tired of taking complaints from patients who felt they were overcharged. However, she quickly found a position teaching fourth grade at Wakefield Elementary School in Fairfax County, Virginia, which she enjoyed.

Ginny almost lost an eye during this period. She came home from work late one evening while snow was falling. She decided to put the car cover on the Renault. In the process, a metal hook slipped from her fingers and hit her eye, shattering her glasses. Almost blinded, she got to a telephone and called Jean Belnap who came to her aid. When I finally arrived, we went to the hospital. The doctor was able to remove all the glass except one small piece which was supposed to work its way out. It never did, and we never used the car cover again.

In the spring, we learned that the people who owned the house were coming back into the area, and we needed to vacate. A friend told us about a house for sale up the street from them. We bought it for $24,000, using a loan of $2,500 from my father for a down payment. In July 1964, I was a happy homeowner.

There was now more time for family activities. Wade went to school two blocks away. Ginny took Billy to school with her, where he started learning gymnastics. Wade played baseball and was a good catcher until another player broke a leg sliding into home plate. Wade felt he was to blame and stopped playing. He was very tender-hearted. We started going to a nearby Methodist Church and spent Sunday afternoons visiting the many sights in the Washington area. We also had several visits from relatives who had not found the opportunity to visit us at previous locations.

Normally, officers working in the Infantry Branch office received whatever assignment they wanted when their three-year tour was over. Mine was over in July 1966. The Vietnam War was heating up. We were sending officers there in advisory roles, and we also had some troop units in-country. Consequently, I was looking at Vietnam as my next assignment. Having missed being in the Korean conflict, I wanted to participate in the Vietnam War.

This was not to be. Several things happened to determine my next assignment. First, I was on that year's list for promotion to lieutenant colonel and was promoted on July 26, 1965. I was selected to attend the six-month Armed Forces Staff College Course in Newport, Virginia. This was a highly desirable course to train officers for joint staff duty. I was delighted to be selected and asked for a subsequent assignment to Vietnam. Since the school was less than a year of duty, it was not considered a change of station; no family move was authorized. Ginny and the boys would remain in Annandale. We were not happy about that.

But one month later, the second event changed everything. I came out on the Army War College list for the 1966–1967 Class. We were elated! This was the Army's top level school. I was to skip the armed forces college-level education and attend the Army War College in my first year of eligibility. Also, it was a year-long course and my family would accompany me.

★★★

The U.S. Army War College was located at Carlisle Barracks in Carlisle, Pennsylvania. The post was built during the Revolutionary War and initially served as an arms depot. It was later used as a government-funded school for selected Native Americans, the most notable being Jim Thorpe, one of the greatest athletes of the twentieth century. The post was small, hosting only the college and necessary support activities such as a commissary, post exchange, and a small hospital. Carlisle was a small town, conducive to family life. We looked forward to a good year. I learned military and political strategies, spent quality time with my family, renewed friendships, and started new ones.

The Army War College was to an army officer what a master's degree program was to a civilian. We studied geopolitics and high-level military strategy. In the process, we mixed with our peers from the Army, other military services, the Defense Department, and the State Department.

It was a gentlemen's course, with lectures from distinguished speakers, papers to write, and a lot of committee work to solve potential world problems. There were no tests. However, we each had a faculty advisor who rendered a performance report on us.

We had ample time to recharge our batteries. Accordingly, Ginny did not teach that year. I tried golf again. It did not work at Fort Benning in 1957, and I wasn't any better in 1966. I switched to working out in the post gym and going bird shooting. The area had corn fields with a large population of dove and pheasant. The student who had the apartment above ours, Colonel Don Doerflen, also liked to hunt. We frequently went bird shooting and took our boys along. I did not get many birds but enjoyed the camaraderie, shooting, and outdoors.

The Steeles and the Doerflens became close friends as well as close in proximity. Noise carried far in the old wooden buildings. Don was a large man, and we could hear him sit down at night in the apartment above and take off his shoes.

Ginny would say, "The second shoe should drop any minute."

We'd wait and then hear the thump of the other shoe.

I think Wade and Bill really enjoyed living in Carlisle. (We had dropped the name Billy at his request.) Twelve-year-old Bill became involved in many teen activities available on the post. Fifteen-year-old Wade had a girlfriend. Although brothers and only three years apart, they were quite different. Wade was still short and stocky, with a quiet personality. He preferred a limited number of friends and spent more time at home. Bill was tall, slim, and outgoing. He made friends easily and was always on the go. Wade was very quick to get angry but equally quick to make up. Bill was slower to get upset but equally slow to reconcile. They got along with each other, disagreeing no more than most siblings did, but they were not close. Nor did they share any friends. At the time, Carlisle was a relatively safe community and both of them had lots of teenage friends and activities from which to choose.

Weekends found us antique hunting, going to the huge local farmer's market, and sightseeing. There was, of course, much socializing with classmates, and Friday night was spent with friends at the Carlisle Barracks Officer's Club.

In early spring, I told Ginny, "Help me decide what my next assignment should be. I really would like to command an infantry battalion in Vietnam. It is our war; our only war. Everything I have done for the last seventeen years has been in preparation for that, and I feel compelled to serve in that capacity."

I didn't expect a positive response and was not surprised.

"I would rather you not go to Vietnam," she replied. "I'm afraid you might get hurt or not come back to us at all. I dread the long year apart and all the worrying it will bring. Having said that, I understand why you want that assignment, and I will support your decision even if I don't like it."

I was assigned to Vietnam but not in a command role. My former boss, Infantry Branch Chief Colonel Don Hickman, was concerned that such a stressful job might be damaging to my heart and that medical aid might not be readily available. I argued my case but to no avail. I contacted one of my former branch associates in Vietnam handling the assignment of incoming officers. He agreed to place me in the 9th Infantry Division. After that, it was up to me to get a battalion. In anticipation of the assignment, I began an increased exercise regimen to include long runs.

Ginny decided that the family would stay in Carlisle while I was in Vietnam rather than go back to our house in Annandale.

"I like living here better than in the Washington area. The boys would not need to change schools again, and they have friends here. Besides, there will be other wives here with husbands in Vietnam, and we can help each other."

I readily agreed and added, "Yes, and people at Carlisle Barracks will be very supportive. I will feel much better with you staying here."

We then presented the idea to both boys. Each responded with a resounding "Yes!"

We moved into an apartment in the same general area and put our house in Annandale up for sale. Ginny quickly lined up a teaching job for the following year. As luck would have it, Jean Belnap moved into the apartment next door.

To refresh me on infantry matters and prepare me for the Vietnam assignment, I was re-blued (blue is the Infantry Branch color) by attending a week-long refresher course at Fort Benning. It was designed especially for infantry lieutenant colonels and colonels headed to Vietnam. We were provided the latest information on enemy weapons and tactics and given a lot of reference material to digest.

My assignment orders authorized thirty days leave after my course ended in late June and set my arrival in Vietnam for late August 1967. We drove to Georgia, spent some time with my parents, and then went to see Ginny's parents who had retired to Florida. While we were there, we visited some of the tourist attractions in the area around Tampa. It was a delightful trip but did little to offset the growing feeling of sadness of my impending departure. Ginny and I both avoided talking about what might happen during that time.

When the day finally came for me to leave, Ginny and the boys took me to Dulles Airport, and we said our goodbyes. Once again, it was extremely difficult and sad. Once again, Ginny was mother, teacher, and family manager. We never became used to being apart.

Ginny and the boys in Annandale with our dog Jackie.

Seeing the Lincoln Memorial in Washington, D.C., 1966.

*Lieutenant Colonel Steele and family at the
Army War College at Carlisle Barracks, 1967.*

CHAPTER 12

5th Infantry Battalion In Vietnam: 1967

My flight to Vietnam took me to San Francisco, and then I traveled by bus to Travis Air Force Base, California. The following day, I joined other replacement personnel on a chartered flight to Saigon with refueling stops in Hawaii and Guam. We arrived very late at night, sleepy and weary. When I stepped from the aircraft, I was immersed in hot, humid air, as though I had walked into a sauna. My first task was to become acclimated.

The next day brought an orientation and the issuance of clothing, equipment and a weapon (a .45 caliber pistol). This was my first opportunity to wear the new lightweight fatigues and jungle boots designed to dry quickly. They proved useful. Then we went to Bearcat, the 9th Infantry Division Base Camp, via helicopter.

I was in luck. The officer handling personnel assignments was someone I knew. He promised to help me get a command. A few days later, I was interviewed by the division commander, then the 3rd Brigade commander, and was subsequently designated to become the next commander of the 5th Battalion (Mechanized), 60th Infantry. The officer originally programmed to take over had been injured which created the opportunity for me to be considered.

The 5th Battalion (Mech) was one of three infantry battalions in the 3rd Brigade, which had responsibility for a large part of the area south of Saigon—an area of low elevation with several rivers, numerous streams, and many rice paddies which provided most of the food for South Vietnam. During the rainy season much of the area was inundated with very muddy water.

The 3rd Brigade headquarters was in Tan An, Long An Province. I was warmly welcomed, was given a few days to talk with the brigade staff, and then accompanied the brigade commander on visits to elements of the brigade.

The battalion commander responsible for the area adjacent to mine was Lieutenant Colonel Dick Zastrow, one of my IOAC classmates. I visited him in his area for two days and learned a lot. I heard my first shot fired in anger there. His base camp came under attack the night I stayed there. However, no lives were lost and no real damage occurred.

The situation and the enemy we faced were unlike a conventional war; it involved counterinsurgency operations. There was an internal struggle for control of the country by a rebel group called the Viet Cong (VC). They were using guerrilla tactics against the South Vietnamese government. This included terrorism of the local populace to gain their support and allegiance. The VC was composed of individuals and small, organized elements that hid among the populace, coming together as needed, to conduct hit-and-run operations against both South Vietnamese and U.S. forces. They wore civilian clothing and were indistinguishable from other citizens. The VC effort to take control of the country was backed by the government of North Vietnam. It wanted to have a single nation under its control. The North Vietnamese provided weapons and other supplies to the VC. In addition, it infiltrated NVA combat units through Cambodia, Laos, and Thailand into South Vietnam to work independently or in conjunction with the VC. It was a complex situation; anyone could be friend or foe at any time.

I took command of the 5th Infantry Battalion (Mechanized) at its base camp in the town of Binh Phuoc on August 28, 1967. It was a long-awaited day, and I felt ready for the challenge and the responsibility.

The battalion with attachments had about 1,000 men. It was equipped with M113 armored personnel carriers (APCs). Therefore, the battalion was more mobile than a regular infantry unit. It could also move by helicopter as the situation dictated. Mobility was essential because our area of operations (AO) covered a large part of Long An Province.

We had several missions: to search out and destroy VC and North Vietnamese forces; to provide security for the civilian populace; to pacify the area of operations; and to conduct independent or combined operations elsewhere in South Vietnam. Because of our mechanized capability, we were also tasked with responsibility for convoy escort along the principal highway connecting Saigon with Can Tho in the southern tip of the country.

The battalion was composed of four rifle companies and a headquarters company that included a reconnaissance platoon, a mortar platoon, a communications platoon, a maintenance section, and a supply section. There were also several attached units—an artillery battery, an engineer platoon, a medical detachment, and a vehicle maintenance support section. It was an effective organization when I took over, and I like to think that it improved over the next six months.

Coordination with the district commander, a captain in the Vietnamese Regional Force, was essential. However, the co-location of my headquarters within his headquarters area was of concern to me. It was on the opposite side of the town from where the rest of the battalion was located. There was only one usable route to get from one side to the other. Therefore, when in base camp, I did not rest easy. Fortunately, we never had a full-scale attack on the headquarters area or the base camp—only harassing mortar fire.

Such coordination, although necessary, also made it difficult to keep our operational plans secret. Whenever we had to coordinate with the Vietnamese district headquarters, we waited until the last possible moment; otherwise someone there might let the VC know about our plans.

Although there was little leisure time, I found time to write to Ginny periodically, and we exchanged audio tapes. We talked together a couple of times when I was in the division base camp and could get to a radio/telephone connection.

I tried to be light as I smiled into the phone. "Hi trooper, how are things on the home front?"

She usually explained what the boys were doing and talked about her efforts to help the other Vietnam widows in her apartment building. Only when time was nearly up did she say, "I miss you and love you. You better come back to us."

"You can count on it," I always said. Somehow, I thought I would.

My mother wrote frequently and often sent cakes and cookies. Some of them melted in the delivery process. She took my going to war very hard, and it may have contributed to her problem with depression. Nothing I said or did helped offset her fear that I might not come back. I believe it worried her more than it did Ginny or me. Her letters usually ended with, "Don't try to do something heroic."

Over the next six months, we stayed very active. Some elements of the battalion were out on a mission almost constantly. On a typical day, one company patrolled our operational area; another was on standby in case contact was made with the enemy; a third company escorted convoys on Highway 4; and the remaining company secured the base camp, worked on a pacification project with the civilian populace, and dried out from being in wet, muddy rice paddies. (The rainy season was underway.)

Unless we were up against a uniformed NVA unit, we could not tell who the enemy was until we saw a weapon and/or it was used against us.

One of the VC tactics was to hide among civilians to avoid detection or to prevent our use of artillery and air strikes on them. Often, we dug them out. In some cases we did dig them out of tunnels in which they were hiding. The courageous soldiers who volunteered for that job were called tunnel rats.

The terrain was very unfriendly. I already mentioned it was inundated by water during the six-month rainy season. Because of that, we had to contend with foot immersion and mosquitoes. Walking in muddy rice paddies meant having to pull your foot out of the sticky mud for each step; walking on the dikes meant risking losing a foot by stepping on a mine. Having wet feet for hours, even days, without care, could put a man out of action. Also, raw buffalo excrement was used as fertilizer. There were frequent stops for foot inspection, foot massage, and dry socks. Each man carried two or three extra pair along with him. Because of the stagnant water, the mosquitoes were huge, came in swarms, and often carried malaria. We combated them with bottles of insect repellent and a daily dose of anti-malaria pills. Leeches were also a problem to contend with. The best way to remove them was to apply heat from a match or cigarette. Just pulling them off could leave part of them inside your skin and cause an infection.

Because of limited ground mobility, the long distances between units, and the short range of radios, command and control (C&C) of operations were more effective from the vantage point of a helicopter. You could see what was happening, move faster, and communicate better. Battalion commanders had full-time use of an H-23 helicopter for C&C. This was a small bubble-top, two-seat aircraft. Whenever some of my units were being airlifted, a larger helicopter was provided (a HU1-D or Huey) for C&C—it had more space and a better radio communications capability. I could take along the operations officer, the fire support co-ordinator, and two radio operators. While in the air, frequently at low altitude, there was concern over ground fire. I usually sat on my protective vest! Though being over the battlefield was the norm, I still spent time on the ground closer to an action to better assess and personally influence the situation.

Early on, I went on several day and night foot patrols. I needed to know what my troops were experiencing as they moved to locate and engage the enemy. That is when I started carrying a folding stock rifle (AR-15) and a large knife in addition to my pistol. I quickly appreciated the difficulty of moving through flooded rice paddies and the dense, tough, and sharp-edged nipa palm bushes growing alongside canals and streams. It was slow going and progress was measured in yards, not miles. I learned to look carefully when using the dikes to avoid stepping on a booby trap or a mine. I also was concerned about sniper fire and that moment of fear when you come under fire and cannot tell exactly where it is coming from. (Do not let anyone tell you they have not been afraid in combat. They have. But most disciplined soldiers control the fear and do what they have been trained to do.)

Frequently, the battalion found the enemy in our AO and we attacked them; sometimes we were sent elsewhere to block or attack enemy forces that were encountered by other units or detected by intelligence-gathering means. On numerous occasions, we took part in brigade-sized operations elsewhere in the delta. (To go into detail about our activities is beyond the scope of this writing. But I will recount some of the actions taken in pursuit of our several missions.)

Mobile Riverine Force (MRF)

Sometimes we operated in conjunction with elements of the 2nd Brigade which was teamed with heavily armed U.S. Navy vessels to form the MRF. This force moved swiftly along rivers and launched attacks against enemy forces detected through electronic intelligence means.

In September, our battalion was assisting the MRF by going into blocking positions inland to intercept retreating enemy units. On the morning of September 12, we heard gunfire when the MRF made contact with the 256th Infantry Battalion of the NVA. My rifle companies were located in positions overwatching large areas planted with rice and interspersed with canals. By mid-afternoon, NVA scouts were noted by our observation posts and skirmishes began in several spots. By late afternoon, we were fully engaged.

I was in a two-seat helicopter (H-23) controlling the ground action and coordinating artillery fires when I saw an NVA unit moving toward the left flank of our position. We needed to get an element to block its movement. When the company commander could not be reached on the radio, I decided to go where I thought he was located. We took fire as the helicopter landed but were not hit. I was able to find one of the unit's platoon leaders, and he moved his platoon into a blocking position and they stopped the NVA unit.

When night fell, the NVA units broke contact and began withdrawing. We continued to place artillery fire and sent out probing patrols. We were not able to make contact again. We accounted for a number of enemy dead, including both uniformed NVA soldiers and VC wearing black pajamas. A number of weapons were also taken. (One of them, a Chinese-made carbine, was given to me when I left the unit. It was on a large wooden plaque with brass plates listing our several large battles.) No one was killed that day, but several were wounded, some seriously.

Ginny listened to the news every day. One morning, she woke to television reports that a mechanized infantry battalion in the Mekong Delta near Cai Lay was in heavy combat with North Vietnam forces. She knew I was in the only mechanized infantry battalion in the Mekong Delta. She started worrying. A friend of ours at Carlisle Barracks also heard it. He called a friend of his at the Pentagon, got the details, and then went to the school where Ginny was teaching to tell her I was all right.

She later told me in a subsequent audio tape, "I was worried about you all morning. And when I saw him coming down the hall, I got a knot in my stomach. I thought he was bringing me a casualty message."

Convoy Security Force (CSF)

Our units providing convoy escort on Highway 4 to and from Saigon were often attacked by small VC elements along the way. They fired a few armor piercing rocket propelled grenades (RPG) at one or more of the vehicles at night, then slipped away before the CSF could react and engage them. Although there might be little or no damage to the convoy, its movement was delayed and the VC would have something to boast about in nearby villages. There was, of course, always the possibility that a larger attack would take place.

This attack came about 2 a.m. one morning in October. The CSF had been hit by a force larger than usual and was moving to engage them. I decided to reinforce with two companies. Helicopters were not available, so we used our APCs and two companies were on the road in thirty minutes.

My first concern was that we might be ambushed along the way. Therefore, I put enough space between the two companies to keep them from being caught in the same ambush. My second concern was that the road might be mined. That was done so often that we swept it for mines daily. Some of the ordinance they used for mines could blow the bottom out of the lightly armored M113 APC, in spite of the sand bags with which we lined the floors. My worst concern, however, was that the CSF might be overwhelmed before we arrived.

But when we arrived, the action was already over. The VC had departed in haste when the CSF brought in artillery fire in preparation for its counterattack. We spent the rest of the night removing damaged vehicles from the road among the swarms of mosquitoes attacking us in the stagnant, muddy rice paddies.

Air Mobile Search and Destroy

In mid-November, we airlifted to the Plain of Reeds (a sparsely populated area with tall reed-like grass mostly inundated by over six inches of water.) We were responding to intelligence that indicated an NVA regimental headquarters was located there.

My plan was to airlift three companies into different spots to locate the NVA units. Company C made contact immediately and the company commander was shot in the chest. His platoon leaders were all new to the unit, so I had the C&C pilot fly us to the tactical command post (TCP), and we picked up my operations officer, Captain Tom Russell. Then, with the help of some suppressing fire from two helicopter gunships (Cobras) and a smoke grenade on the ground to identify the location, we dropped to a hover and exchanged Captain Russell for the wounded officer. As we hovered, we started taking rifle fire. Bullets were hitting the helicopter, and some were ricocheting off the inside bulk-head. The pilot stayed with it, however, until we got the wounded man aboard and lifted off. Fortunately, he lived and except for a few holes in the helicopter, things went well.

Defense of Fire Support Base Cudgel

The next day I was ordered to relieve a rifle company from a sister bat-talion that had been securing an artillery fire support base (FSB) called Cudgel. I sent Company C. This security role was a more stable opera-tion and gave them a chance to dry out. After looking at the size and configuration of the terrain to be secured, I decided to also send the re-con platoon. Because the artillery battery was located adjacent to a canal (the size of a small river), it was exposed to fire from across the bank. The far side of the canal had to be occupied by us. The recon platoon was the elite unit of the battalion, composed of tough, well-trained men who were highly motivated by their platoon leader, Lieutenant Lee Alley. They had been going hard all day. I also chose to locate my TCP there for the night.

After joining them, I gave them their defense orders and then left **to** ensure that the balance of the battalion was set for the evening. When I returned shortly after dark, Captain Russell and Lieutenant Alley re-ported that their units were in position but still digging in. All was quiet and I felt comfortable being with these two units.

However, at 2:30 a.m., we began to receive mortar fire on our position, and the recon platoon began taking mortar and small arms fire. We called for artillery fire and close-air support. The artillery fire came quickly but not soon enough to stop the several waves of enemy troops attacking the platoon. Lieutenant Alley radioed that he could not hold his position on the far side.

I said, "Withdraw and let me know when you are clear!"

Meanwhile, we began to take small arms and rocket grenade fire from all around our position. Although Company C was hit hard, it was holding. I devoted my attention to the recon platoon's situation and began to bring the air support closer to them. We soon started getting fire from directly across the canal, and a mortar round exploded near my side of the TCP. Fortunately, I only suffered ringing in my ears.

I radioed Lieutenant Alley again to determine his situation, and a Vietnamese-speaking voice answered his radio. Lee had either left his radio behind or was out of action. I did not know if all of his men were back on our side of the canal. I had a sinking feeling. I thought, *Should I call in fire on his position now? What if some of his men were still there? Yet I had to act!*

I turned to the artillery forward observer and said, "Have the artillery lower their tubes and fire on the far bank—"

Suddenly, I heard the artillery battery begin firing. (Lieutenant Alley had made it to our side of the canal and ordered the gunners to open fire on the far bank.)

We held our position and secured the artillery battery, but the price was high. Recon suffered the most. Of its thirty-five men, three were killed during the attack and twenty-four were wounded and air evacuated; some later died from their wounds. Only eight men remained for duty in recon after the battle was over.

Many heroic actions took place that night; in my view, Lee Alley's actions were the most notable. His unit took the brunt of the attack. He fought bravely and swam the canal twice to help his wounded men cross to safety. I recommended him for a Medal of Honor, but it was downgraded to a Distinguished Service Cross, the second highest award for bravery.

Lee Alley wrote about his Vietnam experiences in *Back from War: A Quest for Life after Death*. I helped him edit part of the book and also provided a review. His description of the defense of FSB Cudgel was used as my source for the recount of recon's casualties that night.

Counterinsurgency

Much of the time, the Vietnam War was a counterinsurgency action. We were in Vietnam not only to fight and provide security but also to improve the quality of life for the Vietnamese.

We helped construct schoolrooms, playgrounds, bridges, and roads. We provided mobile medical assistance for minor injuries or ailments and gave vaccinations to children. We even provided security elements for farmers while they gathered their rice crop. All of our activities were coordinated with the South Vietnam District Commander and the local village chiefs. Our efforts were well received and most people seemed to trust our motives. However, sometimes the VC entered a village we had helped and tortured or killed several of the villagers to show who ultimately had power over their lives. This negated anything positive we had done, or could do, for them.

The year ended with a sad event. My friend, Lieutenant Colonel Glen Belnap was killed in action a few days before Christmas. While going into one of his company areas at night to coordinate and provide ammunition, the tail rotor of the helicopter he was in struck a tree limb and exploded.

Since army policy permitted the spouse of a deceased soldier to request someone to escort the remains back home and assist during the funeral service, Jean asked for me. I took my friend back home and did what I could to help Jean and her boys through the funeral. Glen's death was a blow to me.

Although my trip home was a somber occasion, it provided an opportunity for me to be with my family for a few days as well as with my parents. Leaving the family for the trip back to Vietnam was just as hard as leaving the first time.

Assuming command of the 5th Battalion (Mechanized), 60th Infantry in Vietnam, 1967.

CHAPTER 13
5th Infantry Battalion In Vietnam: 1968

Shortly after I returned to the battalion, we received an unusual contingency mission. We were to assist the raid of a special forces team on a VC prisoner of war (POW) camp deep in the mangrove swamps at the southern tip of South Vietnam. Twenty-five Americans were thought to be imprisoned there. The scenario for this action could have served as the plot for a war movie.

The plan was for a special forces team to scout the area at night and decide whether to proceed or abort the rescue effort. If it was "go," then a task force from my battalion would be airlifted that night by large helicopters called Chinooks, climb down rope ladders into the target area, join with the special forces team on the ground, hit the POW camp, rescue the prisoners, and extract by helicopter. Because of the density of the large mangrove trees, the assault would be preceded by an Air Force B-52 carpet bomb strike to blow down enough trees so we could hover low enough to get in. We would have to clear a landing area to accomplish our extraction.

We had to be ready for our pickup on short notice. We designated elements to make up our task force, developed our plans, and trained hard for several days, including exiting from Chinooks via rope ladders. On the designated day we waited and waited for word. At 3 a.m. we received word: "no go." The camp was deserted. We were actually disappointed it was called off.

The last few months of my six-month command duty were climatic. On January 31, the North Vietnamese forces broke a cease fire during a significant national holiday called Tet. Simultaneous attacks began throughout the country. It was referred to as the Tet Offensive.

When the Tet Offensive began, my battalion and the rest of the brigade were disposed near the Cambodian border to interdict possible infiltration of NVA units from that direction. My battalion was quickly air-lifted back to our base camp at Binh Phuoc to get our tracked vehicles and resume a mechanized infantry role. Two of my companies were detached from the battalion and attached to the 199th Infantry Brigade, fighting in Saigon. I passed control of them to the 199th commander. He committed them to the fight immediately. I did not like leaving them under someone else's control. I thought, *Will he choose to use my units for the toughest missions?*

I then took the remaining two companies and headed south to clear Highway 4 and assist the South Vietnam units under siege in the city of My Tho. Once the situation was under control there, we set up a perimeter defense and started patrolling the area in an effort to locate any remaining NVA elements. By then, the fighting in Saigon had subsided, and the other two companies rejoined us.

One afternoon, I was airborne in a H-23, listening in on patrol reports. I heard that an NVA soldier had been sighted close to a nearby hamlet. We flew to the area and looked at the hamlet from a distance, as I did not want to alert anyone to our interest in it. It seemed deserted, but figuring that where there was one NVA soldier, there could be many, I decided to obtain more troops. The remainder of the battalion was not far away and could be motorized and on the scene in about thirty minutes. Two companies were instructed to move to the area as soon as possible. The patrol was told to hold up.

When our units got into position, we brought in artillery fire on the hamlet. Right away, NVA soldiers started popping out of the huts, running in every direction. They intended to stay and fight, which was unusual.

I decided to hammer them with air strikes, helicopter gunships, and artillery before making an assault on their positions. We did that for about fifteen minutes. From my vantage point above the area, I was able to locate and mark enemy positions for the air strikes. On one occasion, some tried to get away after a rocket hit near their position. My helicopter pilot took a chance and dropped low enough for me to use my automatic rifle on them. They could not get away as long as we could see them, but night was coming soon. We had to overrun them, or they could slip away in the dark.

I needed to be on the ground. We landed, taking some small arms fire in the process. After a quick planning session with the company commanders, the attack got underway. We drove them back into their secondary positions, but did not break through or cause them to withdraw before dark. We tried to contain them but some escaped. We did not have sufficient troops to adequately encircle the area and prevent them from getting away. But we damaged a company of NVA Infantry that day. Our losses were small, and I attribute that to the extensive use of supporting fires.

Based on what was found, the hamlet had probably been used as a staging area for that unit and others during the Tet Offensive. The area was tunneled and contained supplies, equipment, and a small medical aid station. Obviously, they did not want to give it up.

The U.S. forces won every engagement and killed many during the Tet Offensive. However, the surprise and its magnitude and ferocity severely weakened U.S. public support for the war. This led to the withdrawal of all U.S. forces by the end of 1972.

In late February, it was time for my rest and recuperation (R&R) leave. I left my very capable executive officer, Major Rocco Negris, in charge and flew away to Hawaii. Ginny had already arrived at Fort De Russey in Hawaii to meet me. (Jean Belnap was kind enough to take care of the boys while she was gone.) Ginny was wearing a long, sleeveless, flowered Hawaiian-style dress and a pretty smile. We spent a glorious period together in beautiful Hawaii, staying at the Ilikai Hotel depicted in the 1970s TV program *Hawaii Five-O.*

Being with Ginny again was wonderful. I also appreciated being back in civilization; just flushing a toilet was a great experience! Yet every moment of happiness was tinged with sadness; we faced almost six more months of separation.

When I returned to Vietnam, I was placed on temporary duty as Chief of Staff, 9th Infantry Division Forward CP at Dong Tam. There I would assist Brigadier General Bill Knowlton with the planning for and conducting of operations in the southern part of the division's AO. Rocco Negris would continue as acting commander of the 5th Battalion (Mech) until my scheduled replacement arrived a few days later. That battalion, along with others in the area, would operate under control of General Knowlton and the forward CP.

Just a few nights later, I was awakened by the CP's operations officer.

"Sir, FSB Jaeger is under attack."

That was where Rocco and the 5th Battalion were located!

I rushed to the CP and monitored our efforts to provide support for their defense. Listening to reports and radio traffic that night, knowing it was my unit and my friends in an intense fight, was very emotional. I had confidence in Rocco's ability to handle the fight but felt guilty about not being there with them. I felt like a mother whose children were in trouble, and I was not present to help them. All I could do was monitor the radios and try to expedite the arrival of supporting fires and reinforcements.

They held their ground. Just before dawn, the enemy broke contact and I was able to get into the area. When I arrived, clean-up actions were getting underway. According to Rocco's after-action report, the FSB had twenty personnel killed, sixty-nine wounded, and nine APCs destroyed—two were still burning when I arrived. The canvas blackout curtain between the two battalion CP vehicles still had an unexploded anti-tank rocket just dangling in it. The rocket's malfunction was fortuitous; otherwise the battalion command group could have been put out of action.

The enemy sustained many casualties. The dead North Vietnamese soldiers and their pajama-clad VC supporters were picked up by our troops and grouped together in an open field. I am sure that even more were carried away by the enemy (which was their custom). I was surprised to see several women in the group. They were dressed and armed like men. Many North Vietnamese families probably had no idea what happened to their loved ones who made the trek into South Vietnam.

On March 6, I was officially designated Chief of Staff, 9th Infantry Division Forward CP and served in that capacity until my tour in South Vietnam ended in August 1968.

Given the way in which that war later ended—with the U.S. withdrawal—our efforts were, for the most part, in vain. We lost 58,000 troops in the process. This was sad for our country. From my personal perspective, forty-nine soldiers from the 5th Battalion (Mechanized), 60th

Infantry lost their lives while I was its commander. Many others were seriously wounded. I think of them often and ponder what I might have done differently to prevent their loss.

On the positive side, I was honored to be among a group of wonderful soldiers who did their best to make a difference for the people of South Vietnam and to do their part for their unit and their buddies. I have the deepest respect for the men of the 5th Battalion (Mech) and have kept in touch with some of them.

Although I was not aware of it at the time, one of the lieutenants assigned to my attached artillery battery was Lieutenant Tommy Franks. He went on to become a four star general and commanded the American-led coalition that freed Iraq from the tyranny of Saddam Hussein. Franks wrote a book about his life entitled *American Soldier*. He recounts his experiences with the battalion in Vietnam and mentions my recommendation of Lee Alley for a Medal of Honor.

I became friends with some polite, gracious, and courageous South Vietnamese. Some of those who fought by our side likely suffered after the U.S. withdrawal, including the district commander with whom I worked. I am afraid that he, like many South Vietnamese officials, underwent harsh treatment and "reeducation" by their conquerors from the north; some were even killed.

I humbly received several awards during this time. They were two Silver Stars, a Legion of Merit, a Distinguished Flying Cross, two Bronze

Stars (one for valor and one for achievement), eighteen Air Medals, an Army Commendation Medal, and the Combat Infantry Badge. The government of the Republic of Vietnam awarded me the Gallantry Cross with Palm, the Armed Forces Honor Medal, and the Civil Action Honor Medal.

When the homeward-bound flight took off from Tanh Son Nhut Airport, we clapped loudly. We put the sounds, smells, pain, and heartaches behind us and looked forward to reuniting with our loved ones in the greatest country in the world.

*Receiving Silver Star award from Commanding General,
9th Infantry Division, Major General Julian Ewell, 1968.*

CHAPTER 14

Faculty, Aide, and Brigade Command: 1968–1974

My next assignment was as an instructor on the faculty of the Army War College. In August 1968 we moved into a house at Carlisle Barracks. The boys walked to school, and I walked to work. Ginny continued teaching school. I supervised student committees, had responsibility for teaching one course, and was a faculty advisor for ten students. We had some quality family time, but it did not last long.

In January 1969 I was called for an interview for possible reassignment as aide to the Army Chief of Staff, General William C. Westmoreland. My first interview was with the Secretary of the Army General Staff, Major General Bill Knowlton, for whom I had served in Vietnam. He must have put in a good word for me because, when I met with General Westmoreland, he selected me to be his executive officer and senior aide-de-camp. This was an important assignment as it indicated I was on track to becoming a flag officer (a general). Ginny and I were excited.

But it was certainly not conducive to family life. We had quarters at Fort Myer, Virginia, where General Westmoreland lived, and close to the Pentagon where his office was located. However, the wife of the officer I was replacing would not be moving out until July—four months later. Therefore, I bought a Volkswagen Beetle for transportation and lived in the BOQ at Fort Myer from February until July—another family separation. I was working many weekends and could not get back to Carlisle. Ginny visited me when she could. However, her visits were infrequent because we did not like leaving the boys alone.

As the senior aide, I was responsible for setting the chief's schedule, planning his trips and other activities, screening his correspondence, and supervising his personal staff. I was also the gatekeeper: no one went into his office or called him without going past me. I had to prioritize his time. My work day normally started at 6 a.m. and went until 8 p.m. I carried a beeper and was on call twenty-four hours each day, including weekends, often taking important matters to him late at night. Things happened fast and any actions that had not been handled below the chief's level were usually of major significance. Quite often I had to prioritize actions, quickly absorb the facts and brief him for a decision, then move the action to the appropriate individual or office. I was constantly under pressure and stress to make the "right call." It was nothing like the stress of being in combat but still not conducive to a wholesome family life.

There was, of course, a certain amount of prestige and excitement about my job. It was an important position—one to be envied. General Westmoreland was the top man in the U.S. Army and I was privy to a lot of secret and sensitive information. I was aware of what was going on behind the scenes all over the world. The My Lai story is one example.

While I was there, word that army troops may have killed innocent civilians in the Vietnam village of My Lai surfaced to the chief's office. I saw the Army's quick response with a board of inquiry. I also had an opportunity to see the government at work on foreign affairs and budgetary matters and met many key government officials with whom General Westmoreland came into contact. One of those was Major General Al Haig. He was Special Assistant to Henry Kissinger when he was head of President Nixon's National Security Office from 1969 to 1970. He later served as Nixon's Chief of Staff and as our Secretary of State. Periodically, General Haig came to visit General Westmoreland, and I talked with him while he waited to see the chief. I found him very personable and easy to talk with.

Ginny and I went to receptions given by President and Mrs. Nixon at the White House. We were included in dinners given by Chairman of the Joint Chiefs of Staff General Earle Wheeler and his wife. I had lunch with the President's military aide aboard Air Force One and the *Sequoia* (the President's yacht), as well as in the White House dining room.

Ginny was expected to be available to assist Mrs. Westmoreland "Kitsy" with social affairs. She generously suspended her teaching career. She understood my responsibilities and was very supportive, as always.

★★★

Wade was in his junior year of high school and missed the girlfriend he left in Carlisle. He was in love and tried to keep the long-distance relationship alive by visiting her on a few weekends. It broke Wade's heart when she found someone else.

Bill was a true teenager, and I failed to provide the caring and nurturing he needed during this phase of his life. I exerted more discipline with him than I should have. Long hair was the norm for teenagers then, and I did not approve. Although not to his shoulders, his black hair was at the bottom of his neck.

One evening I looked at his hair and said, "Bill it is time you got a haircut."

He replied "But I like it like this. All of my friends are letting their hair grow longer."

I persisted. "No, it's too long. I don't care what the other boys do. It looks bad to me, and you need to get it cut."

He left the room in a huff and then left the house. He had not returned by bedtime and Ginny was worried.

"Give him time to blow off steam. He'll come home," I said. But he didn't.

She asked, "Maybe you should go look for him?"

"All right," I sighed. "I will, but I don't know where to look."

I drove around the post and the surrounding neighborhoods but did not find him. Returning home, I told a very worried Ginny, "No luck. Let's try to get some sleep. Maybe he will come back in the morning."

Neither of us got much sleep that night. During the long night, I realized how much damage my inflexibility had caused. It also made me aware of how much grief I had caused my parents when I did the same thing over our disagreement about the car.

The next morning, Ginny called me at work. "He showed up at school this morning."

I left work early to talk things over with him. Years later, I learned he had spent the night next door on a couch in a friend's basement! He was smarter than I had been when I ran away.

★★★

I was happy when General Westmoreland asked me where I wanted to go next. I was again thinking about retirement. I longed for a more stable, routine duty that would afford me more family time.

I simply replied, "Fort Benning."

I got the assignment plus the Legion of Merit for my service as his executive officer and senior aide.

Since I had been promoted to full colonel on December 29, 1969 (my second below-the-zone promotion), I was eligible for colonel's quarters at Benning. We chose a large two-story house. I assumed duty as director of the U.S. Army Infantry School (USAIS) leadership department. The goal I set for myself when I entered the Army nineteen years earlier had been attained—I was a colonel assigned to the USAIS. It was a stable and routine job that allowed our family to plan and enjoy more leisure time.

Ginny found a job teaching at Fort Benning. She taught home living at Faith School, not far from where we lived. She loved it and was highly regarded by both teachers and students. She even taught a home living class for boys at their request. Even today, I encounter people she taught who still have fond memories of her.

Wade went to Valdosta State College, a branch of UGA. Because the Vietnam War was still occurring and Wade was likely to be drafted, my father (called Pop by the boys) secured a slot in the National Guard unit in Cordele for Wade. He was required to attend one weekend of training in Cordele each month and two weeks of training at Fort Stewart each summer. Unfortunately, with his college friends and his National Guard buddies, he developed a liking for alcohol that would adversely affect his life.

Bill attended Baker High School with many of his army friends. Racial tensions were intense, and it was an insecure environment not conducive to learning. Bill decided to attend summer school and finish high school early.

He had many friends and spent little time at home. Of course, Ginny always waited for him to get home at night before she went to sleep. We may have given him too much freedom, but he did not get into any serious trouble.

Ginny's parents had sold their house in Vienna and retired to lakeside living in a mobile home near Micanopy, Florida. When we first visited them in the summer of 1967, Mrs. Akin (I always called her that) told us, "That big house was getting too much for us. I told Claude it was time we stopped working and spent some time fishing before we got too old."

Claude added, "We can walk just a few yards, get into our boat, and go fishing in a large lake most every day of the year. Come on, I will show you."

With that, the boys and I joined him for a pleasant afternoon tour of Lake Orange. As we returned, the sun was setting. It was a pretty, tranquil scene.

When we left, I told Ginny's parents. "I can see why you are so happy here. It has given me food for thought."

My mother and father were doing okay, but Mother was still suffering from depression, and my father's drinking had become an everyday occurrence.

On a visit to see them, I told him "Dad, if you want us to come back, you must do something about your drinking problem. I will not expose the boys to it anymore."

Perhaps that had some effect, because not long afterward he had a friend take him to The Anchorage, a rehabilitation facility in Albany, Georgia. It was run by a former pastor, in an old, austere, drafty farm house. Its program was based entirely on belief in and reliance on God. My mother drove there frequently to visit and encourage him. According to her, it was quite cold, and he was very uncomfortable, given his problem and the living conditions. But he stuck it out. Our prayers were answered. The program worked for him. To our knowledge, after his three-month stay there, he never took another drink.

★★★

I enjoyed being in the leadership department. We had responsibility for not only teaching students but also for maintaining army training manuals for leadership, management, physical training, drills, and ceremonies. Our principal subject—leadership—was taught in every course at the USAIS, especially the Officer Candidate Course.

Following the creation of the all-volunteer Army in 1970, the Army established a leadership board led by Lieutenant General Hank Emerson at Fort Bragg. Its purpose was to recommend any changes needed for improvement. Wally Veaudry and I served on the board for four months. While a number of desirable actions resulted, the basic principle remained: leadership principles and techniques did not hinge on whether a person was drafted or volunteered for military service. In either case, troops responded positively to good leadership and negatively to poor leadership. (Time and experience have proven us right.) Several board members received a Meritorious Service Medal for their service during that effort. I was fortunate to be one of them.

Our family discovered the fun of camping in a more comfortable way than the outdoor living a soldier experiences. We purchased a used travel trailer (RV) and took our first trip in February 1971. Bill and two of his friends came with us to the army recreation center in Destin, Florida. We wanted to find somewhere near the beach to leave the trailer and use it like a beach house.

On the way back to Columbus, we went via Panama City Beach, Florida, and found exactly what we were looking for. We were driving down the beach highway and came upon a large, attractive, RV resort that was in the final stages of development. It was called Venture Out. It fronted on the Gulf and backed on the bay; it had varying lot sizes, with concrete drives and patios, all nicely landscaped.

I told Ginny, "This will be great, if we can afford to buy one."

She replied. "Let's find a way." And so we did.

Much of the previous decade we had missed being around our extended family. Now we could take advantage of our close proximity to them. We wanted to visit them frequently and encouraged them to reciprocate.

Ginny's sister, Ruth, and her husband Joe were among the first to visit us. Ruth had retired as a lieutenant colonel (nurse) from the Air Force. Just before she retired, she married an army warrant officer named Joe Jenkins.

I asked Joe, "How did you two meet?"

He replied, "We were stationed in the same area in France, and I met Ruth in the officers' club at the base where she was stationed. I retired a short time later and stuck around to see if I could entice her to retire and marry me."

Ruth finished his explanation. "It didn't take him long. We got married, I retired, and we came back to the states and settled in Dunedin."

Ginny added, "I am so glad. It was time you had a taste of married life." It was obvious to us that they were happy together.

One Sunday in the fall, Ginny planned a reunion with her family at our house. We had the room to entertain and if the weather was nice, we could also be outside.

The weather was warm and sunny. Because of the distance, Mr. and Mrs. Akin came to stay for the entire weekend. While helping them with their luggage, I noticed that Mrs. Akin had a cosmetics case on the floor by her seat. I joked, "Does this contain all your jewelry?"

She laughed and said, "No, this is what I carry our medicine in."

I laughed with her but wondered if I would be doing the same thing one day. Then, it might not be so funny.

Almost everyone came. Ginny spent several days cooking and preparing food, getting the table set for a buffet dinner, and decorating the house in a fall motif. She was in her element and very happy.

She told me, "Please help me greet people when they arrive, and we will gather them for dinner at one o'clock. Everyone should be here by then."

Like a good soldier, I said "Yes ma'am."

As Ginny's family arrived, I enjoyed talking with them. Libby's husband Robert had suffered a stroke and I asked her, "How is Robert getting along?"

With a sigh, she said, "He seems to be able to function well but is unable to work on a job. He has difficulty focusing on anything over a long period of time."

I responded, "How are you doing?"

"I am fine," she said. "I still enjoy teaching in Ware County. Robert takes care of Beth and does the housework for us."

"And the boys?" I added.

"Busier than ever. Bob looks like his father and has lots of girlfriends. Doug has gotten tall and is interested in football. They keep my life interesting."

I reminded Libby how much I appreciated her kindness while Ginny and I were dating.

Ginny's older brother Johnny showed little effects of aging and still had a curly head of hair. I envied him, as mine had thinned considerably. I asked about his family.

He responded, "Edith is fine, still very active. In fact she has an insurance agency in Vienna and doing well with it. Shannon and Reuben are both married and living in Vienna. Reuben retired from the Air Force and is working in Albany. Shannon is farming, building houses, and also working in the insurance business. Life is good."

Bill and Roddy Attaway, Helen's son, were sitting near me while we were eating, and I heard some of their conversation.

Bill asked Roddy what his interests were.

He replied, "I love to play golf and am enjoying high school football in Thomson."

Later, when I mentioned this to his mother, she said, "Yes and he is very good at both." Helen went on to say 'His sister, Rita, is showing her interest in learning. She is getting very good grades in school."

I remarked, "She is also getting sweeter and prettier."

Everyone seemed to enjoy the gathering; we certainly did. That evening Ginny and I were reviewing the day, and I realized I had not had an opportunity to talk individually with her brother R.C. or his wife Allowee.

But Ginny had and she told me, "R.C.'s current job has to do with computers but his hobby is buying and selling used cars. I think he would like to do that full time."

"How about Allowee?"

"Oh, she is working at a department store in Macon and is good at it. I think she should open her own business." She added, "Their son, Allen, is interested in music and playing with a band."

These were the best of times with our families. However, things would soon begin to deteriorate.

★★★

In April 1972, I became secretary of the Infantry School under Brigadier General Bill Richardson, a brilliant, deep-thinking officer, who later became a four star general and commander of the U.S. Army Training and Doctrine Command (TRADOC). As secretary, I monitored the student body, assigned instructors, maintained student grades, supervised the library and bookstore, and handled administrative matters for the assistant commandant. It was an interesting job, and I learned a lot from Bill.

We decided to make a more permanent arrangement at Venture Out. We bought a larger trailer with two slide-outs that expanded outward to enlarge the living area and one bedroom. This trailer was set up on concrete blocks and had a regular ground-mounted air conditioning unit. It provided us a nice vacation home while we were at Fort Benning.

Bill loved the water and learned to water ski. I had thought about having a boat at Venture Out for pleasure and for fishing. We found a nineteen-foot boat (with an inboard motor) that was too appealing to pass up. We parked it in our backyard.

Bill, Ginny, and I took boating classes to become certified to handle a boat. We enjoyed going to the classes together at night. Bill and I were both competitive.

When we started the boating course, he challenged me. "Dad, I bet that I will score higher than you on the final test."

I said, "You are on!"

He got the highest score!

He also became the most frequent user. Two large lakes were near-by—Lake Oliver and Lake Harding—both created by the damming of the Chattahoochee River in Columbus. Bill and his friends went water skiing almost every day while his mother and I worried. That summer, he managed to get a job cutting grass at Venture Out and approached us about spending the summer in the trailer. Of course he wanted the boat and it would be there for us on the weekends. With some reluctance, we agreed. He had a great time; we continued to worry.

Toward the end of the summer in 1972, I arranged for a group of my key officers and their families to spend a weekend at the Fort Benning Recreation Center on the bay in Destin. I thought it would provide a good opportunity for bonding.

It proved to be an eventful weekend. We decided to take our boat but it was still at Venture Out. Major Ken Pond offered to go early and tow the boat over to Destin. He was waiting there when we arrived.

When I thanked Ken for bringing the boat, he responded, "Well I got the boat here but some of the cushions didn't make it. They blew out of the boat on the way over and I didn't realize it."

Oh well, I thought. *How can I fuss at him? He went out of his way to be helpful.*

Early the next morning, Bill and I were putting the boat into the water when it began to sink. Bill yelled, "The drain plug!" He ran to the steering wheel, grabbed the drain plug from a nearby compartment, jumped into the water, dove under, and screwed the plug in before the stern was completely underwater. When he came up dripping wet, he looked up at me and said, "Sorry, I forgot to replace it the last time I cleaned the boat."

I could not chastise him.

The third incident came in the late afternoon. Bill and his girlfriend had taken a small sail boat out into the bay and were becalmed far from shore. There were no motorized boats readily available to tow them in. We decided to let them wait for a passerby to tow them to shore. I worried about them and was prepared to call for a rescue if they did not get in before dark. Fortunately, a passerby soon brought them in okay.

Bill smiled and said, "We really were not in a hurry."

After worrying about Bill, I went to our cabin and found Ginny lying on the sofa. I asked her, "Is dinner ready yet?" (We were having the group in for dinner.)

She replied, "No I am sick on my stomach. I am not sure I can finish cooking it. The shrimp are not even peeled yet."

I ran for culinary help from the ladies in our group. They finished preparing dinner, and Ginny soon recovered.

On Sunday morning, my car would not start; the battery was dead. Someone had a jumper cable and we got the car running. As we were driving home, I suddenly yelled to Ginny, "Something is wrong! I am having trouble steering the car!"

She yelled back, "There goes one of the trailer wheels rolling past us!"

We were not laughing as we pulled over off the road. Fortunately, a Good Samaritan stopped, and we learned there was a trailer repair facility near Eufaula, Alabama. We unhooked the boat trailer, left it and the boat alongside the road, and continued to Columbus in the car. On Monday morning, I arranged for the repair work. It seemed that the wheel had no grease. I believe that was when I thought, *Maybe the time has come to sell the boat.* We sold it that fall.

Wade was in his second year at Valdosta State, and fell in love with Brenda Castleberry from Thomasville, Georgia. The first time he brought Brenda home, Ginny looked puzzled and said to me, "He has not said much about a serious relationship with Brenda. I wonder why he is bringing her home with him?"

"Beats me," I replied. "Maybe he just wants her to meet us and see what an army post is like. Let's see."

We had a pleasant visit with them. I thought about my grandfather who was "little man" to my grandmother. Brenda was slimmer and several inches taller than Wade.

It wasn't long before Wade told us, "Brenda and I want to get married this summer."

My first reaction was, "How are you going to do that and finish college?"

He replied, "She finishes this December and will get a job so that I can finish college." Again, history was repeating itself.

Ginny chimed in, "I am concerned that you don't know each other well enough yet to be sure this is what you want. Why not wait longer to get married?"

Wade persisted, "This is what we both want."

Finally, we acceded but with reservations.

After the Christmas break, Wade left for army basic training at Fort Jackson, South Carolina, which was a requirement of his National Guard commitment. Brenda had no luck finding work in Thomasville and came to live with us in early 1972. (Ginny and I had lived with my parents a few months; my parents lived with their parents for a while; and I suspect my grandparents did also.) It was only natural that we helped Wade and Brenda. She found a job as a legal secretary to the Columbus city attorney while living with us.

When Wade finished training, we went to his graduation parade. He looked great. He had trimmed down and was in the best physical condition he had ever been in—or ever would be in. He was wearing his army-green dress uniform and made a fine-looking soldier. We were all proud of him. Ginny cried. Her little boy had grown into a man.

The wedding date was set for August 26, 1972—Wade's birthday. They had a nice church wedding in Thomasville and all of the Akins attended. We had the rehearsal dinner for them at the Holiday Inn, where most of our family was staying. Ginny cried during the wedding; I knew she would.

She said, "I have lost him now."

I replied, "No, you have gained a daughter." I suspect she was also remembering our wedding. I know I was.

Wade and Brenda spent their honeymoon at Venture Out. They needed an inexpensive honeymoon just like Ginny and I did.

The two of them moved into a mobile home in Columbus financed by my father. Wade continued pursuing his degree in education at Columbus College. He had seen his mother always find work teaching and figured it was a good field.

Bill went to Valdosta State in 1972 but did not like it. After one year, he transferred to Columbus College. This did not work out either. In January 1974 at nineteen and a half years old, he quit college to move to Atlanta with a friend.

Ginny told me, "He called and asked, 'Will you please give me a five hundred dollar loan to get me started?' I went to the bank, had it ready for him, and did not try to change his mind."

Bill told me later, "I think she was ready to cut the apron strings."

Perhaps she was ready to cut him loose, but I know she continued to love him and worry about him.

He worked for a finance company for six months doing debt collections and did construction work during the summer. He finally realized he needed a college degree to get a decent job. In the fall of 1974 he enrolled in DeKalb Junior College. During this time there was little communication between him and us. Yet he was always in our thoughts, and we were concerned about his well-being. Ginny and I knew the dangers and often talked about them.

She said, "What if he gets hurt or sick? What if he tries drugs? What kind of people is he associating with? Will he call us if he needs us?"

I would offer encouragement. "Ginny, he is very self-reliant and hopefully will be guided by the values we tried to instill in him when he was little."

She would counter, "But what if he gets in trouble? Who will help him?"

I did not have the answer.

In early 1973, I was offered command of a mechanized brigade to be activated at Fort Benning in March. I jumped at the chance. This would be a separate brigade with all the elements of a division and could operate independently for short periods without other support. It would be an eighteen month assignment.

My assumption of command ceremony took place on March 21, 1973, on the post parade field. It was the thrill of a lifetime for me, and I was pleased that my family was present. Mom and Dad came over for the occasion.

The best moment was after the ceremony when my dad hugged me tightly and said, "Son, I am very proud of you."

When we got back to our quarters that afternoon, my new command had affixed a large wooden plaque depicting the brigade crest on my front door. I was a happy and grateful soldier!

My mission was to fill the brigade with soldiers and equip and train them to a high level of combat readiness. This was a very exciting and challenging time, and I worked with some wonderful people. The battalion commanders were all first class, and we became close friends. (I am still in touch with two couples—the Hoglans, who live in Niceville, Florida, and the Arneckes, who reside in San Antonio, Texas.) We frequently went to each other's homes on weekends and called our gatherings "Meetings of the 197th Infantry Brigade Board of Directors." We bonded well and this contributed to closer working relationships and a highly proficient unit.

It was a busy period, but Ginny and I managed to spend some weekends at Venture Out. We spent a majority of our time outside on the patio or the beach. We dreamed of retirement and being able to spend long periods of time at Venture Out.

"Ginny, someday we can come here and stay longer than just a weekend; perhaps for a month or more."

"Yes. And we can have everything we need already here so that we can just get in the car and come anytime we like. Furthermore, you will be here long enough to relax and not spend so much time catching up with yard work."

We also continued to make friends there, some of whom are still around. Don and Doris Carmean were two whose company we enjoyed. They also liked RV travel and after retirement, we often traveled with them in our respective motor homes.

By the spring of 1974, my brigade was fully manned, equipped, and trained for combat operations, and we participated in a field exercise against the 82nd Airborne Division at Eglin Air Force Base, Florida. We were there three weeks and had a great maneuver. I was proud of the 197th Brigade; it lived up to its motto "Forever Forward."

I received a call one morning in June 1974 from my boss, the U.S. Armed Forces Command Commander, General Walter T. Kerwin. He said, "Bill, the list of colonels who have been selected for promotion to brigadier general is being released today. You are on it! I wanted to tell you and be the first to congratulate you."

I went directly to Faith School, got Ginny out of her class, and gave her the news. "Ginny, we are on the list for brigadier general!"

Her bright hazel eyes widened and she exclaimed, "How great! I am so happy for you." Then she gave me a hug and a kiss.

We thought about our retirement plans for maybe two seconds and decided to put them on hold.

A relatively small number of officers attain general officer status. I was honored but also in awe of the added responsibility that came with the rank. We heard from friends all around the world, expressing their congratulations and best wishes. However, there was no one any happier than my father.

My mother told me, "I think he told every living soul in Dooly County—some twice!"

Major General Tom Tarpley, the Fort Benning commander, held my promotion ceremony in his conference room with my family and close friends present. It was an impressive room with numerous paintings and infantry artifacts. I had been there for other ceremonial occasions but none as meaningful as this for me. Both boys were there complete with their long hair. Ginny and my father assisted in pinning the stars on me, and I got a hug from each of them. General Tarpley presented me with my one star flag and my leather belt with holster and pistol.

I gave a short speech relating the five points of the stars with the five groups of people who had contributed to my attainment of this level of responsibility. This included my parents, "who gave me the values so necessary for leadership" and my wife and two sons "for their constant and unwavering support for me."

Following the indoor ceremony, we went outside to the parade field for a cannon salute (eleven guns for a brigadier general), and my first review of the troops as a flag officer. The day was sunny and bright but not hot, the band played beautifully, and the troops looked sharp in summer khaki, especially those from the Forever Forward Brigade. The stands were filled with military and civilian friends and supporters.

At the conclusion of the ceremony, the artillery battery commander presented me with the shell casing from the first round fired in my cannon salute. It was a day I shall always remember.

*Ready for a social event while
on faculty of Army War College
at Carlisle Barracks, 1968.*

*With Mrs. Westmoreland during a social
event in Washington, D.C., 1969.*

*With General William C. Westmoreland, Army Chief
of Staff, following my promotion to colonel in 1969.*

William B. Steele Jr.
while attending
Columbus High in 1970.

Social event at the
Infantry School, 1971.

Wade marries Brenda Castleberry, August 26, 1972.
Brenda's mother, Ruby, and her brother, Alva, are on her right.

Major General Tom Tarpley, Commanding General Fort Benning, passes the colors of the 197th Infantry Brigade (Mechanized) to me in 1973.

Completing a brigade morning run
with Brigade Command Sergeant
Major Harvey Parrish.

Private First Class Wade S. Steele
after Basic and Advanced
Infantry Training, 1973.

My parents, Ginny, and me following the ceremony
for my promotion to brigadier general, 1974.

CHAPTER 15

Recruiting Command Fort Sheridan: 1974–1976

Because of the priority given to recruiting of personnel for the all-volunteer Army, two brigadier generals were being added to the U.S. Army Recruiting Command headquarters at Fort Sheridan, Illinois. I was to be one of them. One of my former Vietnam bosses, Bill Fulton, was the recruiting command commander. I was responsible to him for all recruiting operations east of the Mississippi River.

We had acquired three poodles while at Benning, but because we would be in temporary quarters at the Fort Sheridan Officers' Club for several months, we could not have them with us. Captain Jess Brock, one of the officers in the 197th Brigade, and his wife, Marge, asked for them. They loved dogs and were happy when we agreed. It was sad for us, especially Wade, who loved Teenie, the mother of our poodle family.

Fort Sheridan, named for the Union general from the Civil War, was a historic army post located in the suburbs of Chicago, directly on the shore of Lake Michigan. Winters were cold and summers were short (about two months); traffic was always heavy; and it was an expensive place to live. The biggest problem was the distance to our home state and family. Wade was in Columbus, Bill was somewhere in the Atlanta area, and our parents were in Dooly County.

My job involved traveling. It entailed managing a group of sales people who were selling the U. S. Army as a way of life, and we had to achieve monthly recruiting quotas. I traveled from Maine to Florida and from Louisiana to Wisconsin. I spoke to civic groups, motivated recruiters, and made sure they had all the support they needed. Some days I was in two or three different cities. Most of this was accomplished via commercial air. I left on Monday morning, returned on Friday night, caught up with office work on Saturdays, rested on Sunday, and started out again on Monday.

I was also given the task of designing the organizational structure and subsequent implementation of the Military Enlistment Processing Command (MEPCOM) which is still in existence today. New recruits from all branches of the military were sent to an armed forces processing center for physical and mental testing before they were inducted. Each state had one or more of these facilities, located in a major city or cities. These were all staffed and operated by the Army. In 1975, the Defense Department decided to reorganize these under its direct control and staff them with personnel from all services.

Ginny had little to do but chose not to teach in view of disciplinary problems in Chicago-area schools. However, she soon became bored and applied for army civil service work at Fort Sheridan.

When she kept being considered unqualified for the lowest clerical jobs, she started asking, "Why?"

She learned that since I was one of three generals on post, hiring her might be considered nepotism. This was not the case, so I asked the post commander to give her a fair shot at a job. She got a job in the post finance office. They were happy to have her.

Fort Sheridan was a nice place to live. Our quarters were large and overlooked Lake Michigan. The post was small, and everything was within walking distance. We enjoyed socializing with the other two generals and their wives, as well as the recruiting command staff. In addition, we developed friendships with a few civilians in the area and enjoyed some of the fine local restaurants. Ginny loved to shop for antiques, and we spent many Saturday afternoons looking through numerous antique shops.

In the spring, we heard from the Brocks at Fort Benning. They had bred the female puppy we left with them and wanted us to have our pick of the litter. I liked the idea, knowing how much Ginny liked dogs. A dog would be company for her in my absence. When the Brocks offered to bring the dog to us, we quickly agreed. Although we wanted them all, we did not want to disturb their established relationship with the Brocks. We looked forward to the event, as though we were getting another child! We named the female puppy, Cece. Ginny soon decided that Cece needed a male companion and started looking at newspaper ads for poodles. She found some for sale, and we went to look at some. Among the litter were several fine-looking puppies; she picked out the runt of the litter. He came directly to Ginny and started licking her leg. It was love at first sight. I cannot believe I paid $250 for that dog! That was her Pepe. He became Cece's husband and then Gege's father.

Shortly after Christmas, we received a late night call. Ginny's father was in the Augusta hospital. He had leukemia and it had progressed to the final stages. We left that night for Augusta. After several days I had to return to Fort Sheridan, but Ginny stayed in Augusta, along with her sister, Ruth. Claude Akin passed away on February 7, 1975, and I drove back for the funeral. His death was the first we experienced in our immediate family.

While Ginny and I were experiencing some significant life changes, Bill was going through some of his own. He came for a visit during the summer of 1975. At his suggestion, I met him in Atlanta and drove back to Fort Sheridan with him in his Volkswagen. He was cheerful and looked good (although the hair was still a little long). We had lots of time to talk.

Toward the end of the first day together, I commented, "Bill, you seem to be maturing."

"Well, Dad," he replied, "I am getting older."

"Yes, but there is something more."

"I suppose experience has something to do with it. I had to deal with some difficult people working as a debt collector. Construction work involved many tiring days. I'm now convinced that if I want to have a better life, I need to finish my college education."

I responded, "But you are still going to DeKalb Community College aren't you?"

"Yes, Dad, but there is more to it. I have been going to Mount Paran Church with some friends, and I want to go to a college operated by the Church of God to finish up. I have applied and plan to start at Lee College in Cleveland, Tennessee, in the fall."

"Wow!" I said. "That is a pleasant surprise! Your mother and I thought we were remiss in not making Sunday school and church attendance a priority in all of our lives. We regret out decisions and can't offer any excuses. I am so thankful that the Holy Spirit was with you when the time was right. I am delighted! I know she will be happy to hear this news. I must also admit I know very little about the Church of God except that it is very conservative. What will you major in?"

He responded, "Liberal arts."

I concluded our conversation with "Hallelujah!" and "Amen!"

He spent a month with us. It was quality time, but we wished it could be for a longer time. In fact, I introduced him to the daughter of one of my friends. She was close to his age, and I thought that he might extend his stay. He kept to his schedule, though, and all too soon he departed for Georgia. As he drove away, we waved until his car was out of sight. Then I turned to Ginny and said, "I really enjoyed his visit."

She responded, "I agree. It was nice having him here. I have missed him."

"Me too," I agreed. "He has matured considerably and he seems determined to get a degree. Thank goodness."

Ginny echoed my sentiments. "He can do anything he decides to do. He is a man now. But I suppose he and Wade will always be our little boys."

Wade finished college in 1975, and we drove to Columbus for his graduation ceremony. While driving to Georgia, Ginny and I discussed the changes taking place in our family situation.

"Bill," she said. "You and I are entering a phase in our lives when we are the head of our families. Our parents are nearing the end of their lives, and our children are entering the adult stage of theirs. We are in the middle. Our children still need advice and some help, and our parents may also need our support."

"You are so right," I reminisced. "All of our grandparents are gone, too."

I thought to myself, *I still think of them, especially Nanny Steele.* (After living with her son George for a while, she moved into a nursing home to be with her brother Alonzo. Shortly after his death, she passed away with bone cancer at the age of ninety-three, the last of her generation. Her death made me very sad. She was a strong influence on me when I was growing up, and I still think of her often.)

Ginny continued, "Fortunately my father and mother enjoyed a few years in retirement before he died."

I added, "Yes, and it was also fortunate that your sister Helen was able to get them resettled near her. She has been very helpful."

Ginny said, "I think it has made her feel good to be there for them. Now that my father is gone, Helen is in touch with Mother every day, to see what she needs."

I replied. "Being an only child, I may need to do the same for my parents someday. Thankfully, my parents are still in reasonably good health, and Dad can still operate the farm."

When we arrived in Columbus, it was nice see Wade in his cap and gown. He seemed confident and happy. We were proud parents and happy he no longer needed tuition! Unfortunately, he didn't use his training as a teacher. His experience as a student teacher made him realize that teaching was not his forte. Instead, he went into retail sales work.

In 1976, my territory for recruiting duties changed from the eastern to the western part of the United States. During my tour with the recruiting command, I was in each state and most of the major cities in the United States, including Alaska and Hawaii. Ginny went with me whenever her presence supported the purpose of the activity I was attending, and she could get away. She was always ready to go. We had a very nice trip to Puerto Rico and combined a few days of annual leave while there. The nearby island of St. Thomas was a good place to shop for jewelry. (It turned out to be an expensive trip.) Another nice occasion was a weekend in Michigan, as Grand Marshall for the Apple Blossom Festival. We were wined, dined, and well treated.

I was on the promotion list to major general that was announced in June 1976. I longed to return to troop duty and spoke to the Army Chief of Staff, General Bernie Rogers. Subsequently, I was assigned as commanding general of the 5th Infantry Division (Mechanized), soon to be activated at Fort Polk, Louisiana. I was elated!

Sadly, Ginny's sister, Ruth, died an early death in August 1976 at age fifty-four. (While she and Ginny were in Augusta with their father, she went to the army hospital in Augusta, ostensibly for a routine physical, but she had throat cancer. She kept it from everyone except her husband. Ruth was the first sibling to die of cancer; there would be others.)

My promotion took place in September, and my parents came to Fort Sheridan for the occasion. It was the only time they visited us there. Neither of them liked to leave home nor did they like to fly. I was especially pleased and honored to have them present. They both looked good. Mother was still pretty, although her figure was a little larger. I was pleased to see that my dad was still staying away from alcohol. Unfortunately, this would be the last time they were able to participate in something like this, and it provided a good memory.

*Brigadier general and deputy commander of
the U.S. Army recruiting command, 1974.*

*Major General Eugene Forrester and
Ginny pin on my second star, 1976.*

Mom and Dad attend the promotion party
in our quarters at Fort Sheridan, 1976.

CHAPTER 16

5th Infantry Division And Fort Polk: 1976–1978

We moved to Fort Polk in November 1976, and there were two major missions: to organize, equip, and train the 5th Infantry Division (Mechanized) for reinforcement in Europe; and to construct new facilities on the post.

These were not small tasks. A mechanized infantry division consisted of approximately 18,000 men and women, plus thousands of vehicles and pieces of equipment. It was composed of many diverse units, requiring a tremendous amount of training to be an effective fighting force. Converting Fort Polk from a World War II post of wooden structures into a modern brick and mortar military installation, including 3,000 new family quarters, was a monumental undertaking. Both missions were to be accomplished simultaneously.

For the second time, I left Ginny with the job of moving in by herself. The U.S. Army commander in Europe scheduled an orientation tour for the division commanders who provided reinforcement units for him if the "balloon went up." (This meant the Soviet forces were attacking with or without nuclear weapons.) I departed for Germany the morning our household goods arrived. Ginny was amazing. She figured out how to move furniture by herself by putting a blanket under the legs and pulling the furniture into place.

My priorities were to transition the installation from an infantry basic training role and its philosophy, usher in a new group of people, and start the flow of equipment and facilities to support the division's growth. The days were long but exciting and rewarding. By spring of 1977, we were at full strength and had enough vehicles and equipment to begin unit-level training. We also observed new construction around the main post area. Coordination with the army civil engineers on construction matters became an increasingly important requirement for me. Ginny stayed busy as well, working to develop the network of wives activities necessary for the support of family needs and morale.

She was also interested in influencing the layout and decorative features of the family housing under construction. At one ground breaking ceremony, I was presented with a construction area hard hat complete with two stars while they gave Ginny one with three stars!

Due to the organizational structure of the division, we had contact with people throughout Louisiana. The 256th Infantry Brigade (Mechanized), a unit of the Louisiana National Guard, was designated as one of my brigades in case of deployment. It would round out the division's organizational structure. Consequently, I had an interest in their state of readiness and spent lots of time visiting the 256th Brigade's units. Unfortunately, our only chance to train with them was when they assembled at Fort Polk for their two weeks of summer training.

All was not just work, however. We encouraged unit social functions, and we attended many. We also entertained the commanders and the division staff and got together with them in small groups. In addition, we participated in numerous civilian activities in the surrounding communities of Leesville, DeRidder, and Alexandria. We developed some close friendships that have lasted for many years. As the senior army officer in Louisiana, there were frequent requests for me to attend and speak at community functions. Ginny went with me whenever she could. The Cajun people in Louisiana loved to celebrate and used any excuse to do so. Thus we enjoyed lots of crawfish and crab boils, accompanied by Cajun music.

Division commanders had always been authorized an enlisted household aide who cooked. However, that perk was being deleted when I arrived at Fort Polk. Ginny prepared everything when we entertained military and civilian groups. We did hire a server from the officers' club staff to help during some events, but it was still very hard on Ginny. To her credit, she never complained.

In the fall of 1977, we received relief. My boss, General Fritz Kroesen, headquartered at Fort McPherson, visited to see how the division was progressing. We had a dinner party for him and invited about thirty military and local civilian leaders to meet him.

During the dinner, he asked me, "Who prepared everything?"

I told him, "Ginny. I hired a woman from the officers' club staff to help serve dinner."

The next morning, his aide called me. "General Kroesen just called the army staff and told them to authorize an enlisted aide for you immediately."

We started interviewing cooks and soon found a great one: Master Sergeant Joe Cline.

We had other visitors, including family members. Ginny's sister, Libby, came for a week. Ginny was delighted and suggested, "Bill, let's take a few days off and show her some of Louisiana."

I replied, "Okay, let me see what I can do."

I called the state adjutant general who controlled the 256th Brigade. "I am taking a relative to New Orleans for a few days," I said. "Where is a good place to stay?"

He responded, "We have a state-owned visitor's house in town. You can use it."

We toured southern Louisiana, ending our week in New Orleans.

When Libby departed, she told us, "This was the best trip I have ever had."

My parents were not able to visit us at Fort Polk. While we were there, I found out Dad had leukemia.

I immediately called Ginny with the news. "My dad has cancer."

She asked, "When? How did he find out about it?"

"It was detected in a routine blood test," I said. "It is leukemia."

She said, "I am devastated. I don't know what to say."

I echoed her thoughts. "Ginny, I just never considered him having cancer. He is not old yet! I am stunned and having a hard time dealing with it. We are so far away from him. How can I be there for him and support him?"

★★★

In the fall of 1977, the division was designated to participate in a major army exercise, which served as a rehearsal for wartime reinforcement of U.S. Army Europe. It was called REFORGER 78 (reinforcement of forces in Germany in 1978). The exercise involved the movement of a division, plus combat support units, to Germany where the force would retrieve pre-positioned heavy equipment, move to defensive positions, and maneuver against another division-sized unit. (A substitute unit was provided for the 256th Infantry Brigade which could not go with us.) The actual field exercise lasted about three weeks but the total involvement time was closer to eight weeks. My headquarters coordinated the movement of all forces deployed from the continental United States to Europe. They were all under my command while we were outside the United States. Much had to be done to prepare, and we had until October 1978 to get ready. Fortunately, we had some outstanding brigade commanders and staff officers. Everyone went to work. We pressured our higher headquarters to provide the remaining personnel and equipment needed to flesh out the division in time to conduct the necessary training. We also stayed in constant contact with the accompanying units and those who would be transporting us. There were a myriad of plans and details to be worked out. In addition, I or members of the division staff had to visit the various units to ensure everything was going according to plan. I planned to minimize my time away from Fort Polk until the overseas movement began. Then I wanted to be in Europe when the units started arriving.

In the midst of this planning, Wade and Brenda were expecting a child in April. Ginny and I went to Columbus as soon as we heard Brenda had gone into labor. When we got there, Brian had already arrived. We were grandparents! We went directly to Brenda's room. I think my first act was to look at Brian and then say to Ginny, "What a good-looking boy!"

Then I remembered his mother. I turned to Brenda and said, "Thank you for giving us a beautiful grandson. Are you all right? Can I hold him?" I had not had the opportunity to hold his father when he was newly born.

As I recall, she replied, "I am fine and yes, you may hold him." After a few minutes, Ginny tugged on my arm and whispered, "I know this is just wonderful, but now it is my turn to hold him."

A few minutes later, the hospital room telephone rang. It was my aide, Captain Buff Blount. "Sir, the Secretary of the Army wants to interview you tomorrow afternoon for possible assignment as commander of the Army Recruiting Command."

While consideration for this high priority position was flattering and might lead to a third star, it was not one I wanted. I did not relish thoughts of the constant travel associated with the recruiting command responsibility. But I had to go for the interview.

On arrival, I found that two of us were being interviewed. My chance of being selected was fifty percent. I felt a little better.

The secretary was direct. He asked, "What do you think about the recruiting command?"

I replied, "Sir, it is an important job and one I am familiar with. If you decide that you want me in that position, I will give it my all. But it is not a position that I would seek."

He told both of us that we would get an answer in a few days.

That night I called Ginny. She was staying with Dick and Sally Zastrow (friends from my IOAC and Vietnam days), checking on our rental house that we had purchased as a possible retirement home.

I brought her up to date on my interview and said, "Maybe events of the past few days are indications that it is time we made a change. We now have a grandson, my father has leukemia, my mother is suffering from depression, and neither of us wants the separation that a recruiting command assignment or possibly an unaccompanied overseas assignment will bring. Also, our house in Columbus is currently unoccupied."

She responded. "Those are all good points, and we have been leaning toward retirement for some time. Perhaps now is the time."

I replied, "Let's sleep on it and discuss it further when I get back to Columbus tomorrow."

The next afternoon, we reviewed our options again and decided to retire from the Army as soon as possible, move to Columbus, work there for a few years, and then fully retire. We had spent years away from family and wanted to see our grandchildren grow up. We both were ready to settle somewhere, and Columbus was a good place to do so. We were comfortable with our decision.

Ginny then showed she was ahead of me again. She gave me her brightest smile and said, "After looking at our retirement house, I have changed my mind. Although it is a nice house in a very nice area, it is larger than we need and has two stories. We need a smaller, more modern house on one level."

I protested, "But we bought that house with retirement in mind. Besides, think of the cost. We don't have the money to buy a new house."

She was prepared for that argument. "Yes we can. Dick thinks we can sell that house and clear enough for a good down payment on building a house in a new subdivision called Beaver Run. It is on the northeast side of Columbus. We have been looking at areas and houses since yesterday morning, and I like that subdivision."

I trusted her judgment. "Show me."

By late afternoon, we had picked a lot, selected a floor plan, and signed a contract with a builder. Dick agreed to check on the construction periodically, and we headed back to Fort Polk.

The next day I sent a backchannel (secure) message to the Army Chief of Staff. "Respectfully request to be placed on retired status as soon as possible. Consideration for the recruiting command assignment has caused me to realize the need to reprioritize my time to meet family care needs and desires at this point in my life. Therefore, I wish to retire and make room for someone else."

The Chief of Staff asked me to reconsider. I did not. The decision had been made. This was one of the most difficult personal decisions I had ever made.

In my mind, I would ask the question, What if I had stayed? numerous times.

The chief agreed to my request but asked me to remain until after the REFORGER 78 exercise was completed. We pushed the builder to get our house finished by August so we could move into it before I departed for the exercise in Germany. Ginny would get settled while I was gone (imagine that), and then go back to Fort Polk when I returned in November. We would depart Fort Polk in December. I planned to take annual leave until my retirement date: January 1, 1979. On that date, I qualified for retirement pay based on twenty-nine years of army service and seventy-two and a half percent of my annual salary, adjusted annually by inflation.

✯✯✯

Bill came to visit us in July 1978. While admiring the new Fiat convertible sports car he drove up in, I said, "Bill, this is a sporty set of wheels. How can you afford it?"

He replied, "A very long-term loan with small payments."

I quickly added, "You sure can't carry much luggage."

He smiled brightly, a little like his mother, and countered, "I travel light."

I knew when to quit! While he was there, he joined me for morning runs, and I took great pleasure showing him the post and introducing him to everyone we met. All too soon, we were waving goodbye as he drove off in his sports car.

As the summer progressed, the tempo picked up. I was busy with training and field exercises, trying to get the division ready to maneuver against a well-trained army division in Germany. Ginny and I were also making modifications to our house plans and tracking the progress of its construction long distance. (This is not recommended.)

Once the movement phase of REFORGER 78 got underway, we had people and equipment flowing into Germany, the Netherlands, and Belgium from all parts of the United States. This entire process took about two weeks and included the time required to obtain tanks and other heavy equipment pre-positioned in German depots and drive them to the assembly areas. I went to Europe and met many of the units as they arrived. When my staff and I arrived at Rhein-Main Airport in Frankfurt, Germany, there was an arrival ceremony with a welcome by the commanding general of the U.S. Army Europe, along with NATO officials and a number of German dignitaries.

We had a formidable force and were in our initial field defensive positions on the scheduled date. Our mission was to delay the enemy's advance until more units arrived from the United States. We did that for two weeks, counterattacking whenever the opportunity arose and gave up very little ground.

Because of the way our forces were positioned one night, we saw an opportunity to inflict a lot of damage to the opposing force. We moved a tank-heavy force that night across our thirty-five-mile front so we could attack on both flanks while holding in the center with a lighter force. It worked and caused the umpires to terminate the exercise early in our favor. I savored every moment of the exercise critique the next day. A newly activated division had beaten an experienced NATO division in its own backyard. I was so proud of my entire force. Thankfully, the entire exercise was accomplished without any loss of lives.

After the maneuver phase, we cleaned and returned equipment to the pre-position sites, gave the troops a week off to enjoy the local sights, and then watched over the unit's return to the United States.

I spent my last few days at Fort Polk resting, cleaning up loose ends, saying goodbyes, and getting ready to turn over the division and the post to my replacement.

Every unit of the division was represented in the change of command ceremony when I relinquished command to Major General Joe Palastra, later a four star general and commander of the U.S. Army Forces Command. The day was cool, crisp, and sunny; a perfect day for a ceremonial review. There were thousands of soldiers, all very sharp in their battle dress. There were a number of tanks and other armored vehicles. The band played beautifully, and there was a helicopter fly over. The stands were full of well-wishers, including Bob and Mimi Gillespie, friends from the Fort Sheridan days. The forces command commander conducted the change of command ceremony and presented me with a Distinguished Service Medal. Then the troops passed in review. I had trouble suppressing my tears. I lost it when the last man in line approached. It was a lone second lieutenant, carrying a flag staff with a blue flag showing the designation of the first unit in which I served— Company A of the 1st Battalion, 22nd Infantry Regiment. Following the ceremony, after saying our final goodbyes, Ginny and I drove away. Neither of us said anything for quite a few miles.

While my army life was over, I would not be officially retired from the Army until January 1, 1979. I would be on leave status until then.

Therefore, my actual retirement ceremony was conducted at Fort Benning, where it all began, by another former IOAC classmate, Major General Bill Livsey, who was commander of the Infantry Center.

Each major unit at Fort Polk had given me a gift, and we had to find a place for every gift. For lack of space inside the house, we put the overflow of plaques and pictures on the walls of the garage. Whenever I drove into the garage, I was happy to see them.

One item went into the den. It was an overstuffed chair with infantry-blue upholstery decorated with a two-star headrest, in and out pouches on the armrests, and a bell on one armrest for use in summoning an aide. Ginny quickly let it be known that there would be no response to the bell. Yes, I removed it immediately. My army life really was over!

At Fort Polk (from left to right): Anita Blount; my aide, Captain Buff Blount; my secretary, Dianne Penney; me; and Ginny, 1977.

Presentation of the arriving REFORGER 78 forces to the NATO commander at the Rhein-Main Airport in Germany, 1978.

With Ginny and friend Mimi Gillespie following my departure ceremony from the 5th Infantry Division (Mechanized) and Fort Polk, December 1978.

*Major General Bill Livesy, Commanding General, U.S. Army Infantry Center,
presides at my retirement ceremony at Fort Benning, January 1979.*

CHAPTER 17

Aflac–United States: 1979–1988

Although I retired from the Army in January 1979, I intended to continue working in some capacity. Shortly after tendering my intent to retire, I started sending resumes to businesses in Columbus hoping to go directly to a civilian job.

It did not work out that way. The responses to my job search were disappointing.

"There are no vacancies for someone of your qualifications."

"We prefer to promote from within."

"You are overqualified."

"You are accustomed to giving orders and might have difficulty taking them."

Ginny and I both thought the real estate business might be interesting, and we could work together. Also, commission-based, sales jobs were more readily available. She qualified for her license in January and went to work as an agent in the brokerage where Dick Zastrow was located. In January, I started studying for a license but continued my search for other work, too.

I investigated the requirements for a teaching position. With just a few courses, I could get certified to teach in high school—history or civics. Because I was eligible for the Veteran's Education Funding Bill (the

GI Bill), I decided to take some courses at Columbus College. I did some substitute teaching in economics at the Chattahoochee Valley Community College. That helped with our finances, but I was depressed over my lack of a job and the erosion of our savings.

In the spring of 1979, Bill came to visit us. Since dropping out of the seminary in 1977, he had been coaching gymnastics in Louisville, Kentucky. He did well coaching college-level women gymnastic teams that won championships. He believed there was a market for a gymnastic school in Columbus and wanted to move there. He asked for our help financially and we agreed. We were delighted that he moved to Columbus and believed he could make his idea come to fruition.

His arrival in Columbus coincided with Wade's move to LaGrange, Georgia. Wade was selling life insurance on a debit basis like Brenda. They worked existing business to collect premiums, sell additional policies, and get referrals for new prospects. Brenda was one of her company's top sales people and thought Wade would also be successful selling insurance. He was a natural salesman—warm, personable, sincere, and attentive to customers' needs. He did so well that in 1979 he was offered a managerial opening in LaGrange. Ginny used her real estate experience to find them a nice house. We bought it and let them make the payments until they could own it.

Bill's business, Gymnastics Plus, was a tremendous success. Ginny located a building for him, and I provided some business expertise. Bill did most of the work himself, including: making equipment and finding used equipment; remodeling the interior; planning class schedules; and hiring part-time instructors. He also became partners with a woman who had been teaching high school cheerleading. By the time Gymnastics Plus opened in the summer, hundreds had enrolled, and the school was off to a great start. We were impressed with what he was able to accomplish in a short time and with limited funding.

By early summer, Ginny had become unhappy with the real estate business. She had sold only one house and was not enjoying the work. She applied for a civil service job at Fort Benning and got it right away. She could always find a job!

My opportunity came in August. I had rejoined the Kiwanis Club, having been a member when we were at Fort Benning in the early 1970s. At one of their lunch meetings, I sat across the table from Pete Morrow, the marketing director of Aflac (American Family Life Assurance Corporation).

During our conversation, I said, "Although I have retired from the Army, I am not ready to stop work. Unfortunately, the job market in Columbus is limited for upper-level management. Most employers do not believe I would be happy doing something at a lower level. They are wrong. I am willing to enter at any level and prove my worth for higher levels."

He responded, "If anything opens up, I will consider you."

A few weeks later, he called. "Bill," he said. "I have an opening that might interest you. It doesn't pay much but you will have an office and a secretary, and it will give you something to do. It involves planning and conducting award trips for sales contest winners."

I said, "Yes!" Aflac was a large, growing corporation and this gave me an opportunity to grow with it.

After interviews with my prospective boss, Pat Stubbs, I was hired.

Pat later told me that she knew we could work together from my response to one of her questions.

She had asked, "How do you feel about working for a woman?"

I responded, "Fine. My best friend is a woman."

I was comfortable in my new job. I was responsible for sales award trips, handling occasional visitors, and conducting sales training courses for several nearby states. I had to plan, coordinate, and follow-up on all activities to ensure things went well. Some writing and speaking were involved. I was well versed in these things and was familiar with sales management, having majored in marketing at UGA. Of course, I had to learn about the principles of insurance and the jargon used in the financial industry.

The job kept me busy but was much less stressful than my previous work. I was happy to be working again and found the environment very pleasant and rewarding. Scouting destinations for annual sales award trips was especially nice. Ginny was often able to accompany me and provide a spouse's viewpoint. We also attended the events to ensure that everything went as planned. Although they were working trips for me, there were many opportunities for us to be together during the trip. Since these were award trips for sales excellence, everything was done in a first-class manner—much nicer amenities than what we had been accustomed to in the past.

Our first taste of that was in October when Ginny and I were guests at an Aflac annual sales convention in Los Angeles, California. We went as guests but it really served as a training exercise for us. We stayed at the Bonaventure Hotel and had a whirlwind tour of all the local attractions including Hollywood, the movie studios, and Disneyland. Evenings were filled with fine dinners, awards, and entertainers. It was designed to reward top sales leaders and motivate them for the next year's effort. It served its purpose. It was certainly exciting for the two of us, especially when the shark from the movie Jaws jumped out of the water by us at Paramount Studios—Ginny jumped into my arms!

Another interesting occasion was an awards trip to New York City in January 1980. We stayed at the renowned Waldorf Astoria Hotel. While planning for the meals there, I asked the hotel representative, "Can you have a southern-style breakfast the first morning and include grits?" (Many of our trip winners were from the southern states, and I wanted to surprise them with grits for breakfast during their stay in the

North.)

He hesitated for a moment then said, "Yes. I think we can find some grits."

When breakfast began, I was surprised when the waiters marched in. They served everyone a large cereal bowl filled with grits! Obviously I should have been more specific with my explanation that we eat our grits on a plate with our bacon and eggs.

We also did some traveling for pleasure with our army friends. The local Retired Officers Association chapter arranged group trips. One of the trips we enjoyed most was to Branson, Missouri. We were there in November, and all the shows were decorated for Christmas. Andy Williams was fantastic and despite his age, he was still a great singer. Perhaps I was influenced by the fact that his style of music is my kind of music!

★★★

Ginny and I were in San Juan, Puerto Rico, for an Aflac annual sales award trip in May 1980 when I noticed the phone message light blinking in our hotel room. Dad had contracted pneumonia and because of his weakened condition from leukemia and the chemotherapy, he was not expected to live.

Ginny and I dropped everything and rushed to catch the last flight home that night. Dad and I had a little time together before he died at 3:30 a.m. on May 26. I was thankful that I arrived in time to tell him again that I loved him and to be with him when he died.

I was also thankful that my early retirement enabled me to have nearly two years to see him more often and help him to and from chemotherapy treatments. During those trips we became closer than we had ever been, and it was a blessing for me.

My mother would not be able to stay on the farm alone. We wanted her to be near us. Having lived with her mother-in-law on two occasions, she preferred her independence. But she could no longer drive. Therefore, we found her an apartment in the Windsor Park area next to a shopping center. She could easily walk to a grocery store, a drug store, and a beauty shop. We took her anywhere else she needed to go.

Things went well for a time but nothing we did could take the place of the companion she had lost. She continued to be depressed. Ginny and I spent time with her often, and I had lunch with her almost weekly. She delighted in cooking country-style meals for us and never lost her ability to do it well.

Elizabeth Lewis, our housekeeper at Fort Benning, was still in the area. She soon started working for us two days a week and eventually began helping my mother one day a week, too.

In the summer of 1980, I was promoted to vice president for national training and recruiting. I was responsible for creating a new department, implementing a national program for training of sales coordinators, and recruiting sales agents. We rolled the program out in December 1980, and it was a success. By the end of 1981, we had conducted training for all of the sales coordinators and assisted with recruiting efforts in most of the states. In 1982 we started helping our sales force gain access to Japanese-owned companies operating in the United States. On July 21, 1982, I accompanied a senior member of our Japan branch to San Francisco to meet our state sales coordinator and get the program underway in California. When the plane landed in San Francisco, I received devastating news.

My mother was dead. She had died in her sleep. Bill found her in bed after the neighbors did not see her that morning. It was difficult for him but he handled it well.

I believe I cried all the way back from San Francisco. Her passing affected me greatly. We had always been close. I appreciated her love for me and prayed that she knew how much I loved her. We took her back to Lilly for the funeral and buried her next to my dad on July 23, 1982. Somehow, with Ginny's help, I got through the service. Now my parents and grandparents were gone. It was sad and depressing.

Probating my mother's will was easy because of my father's foresight to transfer his estate and reduce the tax burden. He had transferred the farm to me and my family several years earlier.

He began the process in 1973, gifting the maximum annual tax-exempt dollar amount of land to Ginny and me over several years. He gave some to Wade and Bill to complete the transfer sooner, too. Dad placed only one stipulation.

"Do not sell the farm."

Ginny and I were humbled by what he did. He knew we would care for his needs.

We set up Steele Investments, Inc. and Jacob Beil, our attorney, exchanged our portions of the farmland for shares of stock in the corporation. I have valued his wise counsel for many years.

Over time, we have expanded the corporation's interests to other investments. But its primary financial benefit remains rental income from the farmland.

After the death of my mother, Ginny and I realized Wade had a drinking problem like my dad. Wade was like my father in several other ways. As with Dad, Wade was friendly and everyone liked him, but he could be stubborn and hardheaded.

Meanwhile, through a mutual friend, Bill met Debbie Skarpness at Gymnastics Plus in 1980. She had completed her associate's degree in nursing and was moving to Augusta to work on her bachelor's degree. She and Bill decided to get married in December, 1981. They gave us only a few weeks' notice, but somehow all arrangements were accomplished and everything worked out well. The wedding reception was held at our house. It was a festive day, and we were happy that Bill had someone to share his life. We also might have more grandchildren!

I took a picture of Debbie dressed in her wedding gown holding a baby. I jokingly told Ginny, "Someone seeing this picture may think that the baby was Debbie's."

She replied, "Thank goodness it isn't."

Actually, the baby she held was Wade and Brenda's second child, Marie Shannon, who had just been born on December 1, 1981. She was a precious baby.

Bill and Debbie moved into a house we purchased for them with the same rent/ownership plan we had for Wade and Brenda. With Debbie's encouragement, Bill started rethinking his purpose in life and decided to resume his path to the ministry. As a result, in December 1982 he sold the gymnastics school and they moved to Louisville. He reentered the Baptist seminary in January 1983. Debbie also took some courses at the seminary while they were there. Ginny and I were sad to see them leave Columbus but happy over their decision to seek a life in the ministry.

Wade's alcoholism worsened, and he lost his managerial job. He and his family moved back to Columbus. In the fall of 1982, shortly after their move to Columbus, Brenda came to me about Wade's drinking problem. It was seriously affecting their family life. I had lengthy discussions with Wade but to no avail. By June 1983 the situation became intolerable for Brenda and the children, so she took the children and moved to Phenix City, Alabama, without him. I understood what she did and fully supported her decision. I was concerned for the children's welfare and also hoped it would motivate Wade to quit drinking. Ginny and I let Wade move in with us on a temporary basis, and we got him into the first of a series of rehabilitation efforts.

I connected him with a local Aflac district sales coordinator, leased a car for his use, and prayed he would overcome his problem with alcohol. He did not change. On return from a weekend Aflac trip, we found him in jail. He had been drunk and had a vehicle accident. I bailed him out, went to court with him, and paid his fine, knowing that I was continuing to enable his behavior. We knew, of course, that we could not induce a behavioral change. He had to do that himself. He found a job in Success Dress, a men's clothing store, owned by Forest Colson. Forest was a reformed alcoholic and strong disciplinarian. He was very good for Wade. We leased Wade an apartment near where he was working and provided the minimal amount of furniture. We also got him a bicycle to get to and from work since his driver's license was suspended.

For a while we thought Wade was improving but then he met Kathan Bettin. She was a divorcée who lived in the same apartment complex. She had two teen-aged children, a boy and a girl. Wade started seeing her and later married her in spite of our protestations. With his addiction, Wade was in no position to assume added responsibilities. I did not think Kathan would be a strong motivating force for him to stop drinking, and she had problems with her legs, which eventually caused her to be unable to work. Wade sank further into alcoholism and the resultant difficulties.

One of my last tasks in the Marketing Department was to develop a special policy for use in a sales presentation to a group of people in Madrid, Spain. We were not successful but while we were there, I left my wallet in a taxi.

I called Ginny. "Honey, I just did the dumbest thing. I left my wallet in the backseat of a cab in Madrid."

She said, "Call the cab company."

"This is Spain. "I don't even know the name of the company. I think the taxi driver is independent. I don't know how to get in touch with him. He is probably off spending my money now. I need you to cancel our credit cards. It will take me forever to do it from here."

She replied. "Okay, but what will you do for money?"

"I will find an American Express office and get an advance on my account."

Just then, someone knocked on my door. Who was that? I wondered.

I opened the door and there stood my cab driver.

"Senor," he said. He held up my wallet. "Is this yours?"

I felt surprise, disbelief, and elation, all at the same time.

I cried out, "Yes!"

He continued in very broken English and sign language.

I interpreted his English and sign language to say, "Next man find in seat. Hotel give room."

He handed me the wallet and I looked inside. My money and credit cards were still there. Nothing was missing.

I said, "Thank you. I am very grateful to you. You are very kind. Let me hire you for the entire day tomorrow, and you can show me the city."

We had a great time, and I rewarded him well. At the end of the day, he took me to meet his family and I took them to dinner. I realized there were still honest people in the world.

In 1984, as the result of a study I did regarding the conservation of Aflac insurance policy holders, I was reassigned from marketing to administration and given the task of organizing and managing the conservation department. I was elated. The new position necessitated very little business travel.

But Ginny and I did make a trip to greet our third grandchild. Bill and Debbie gave birth to William Berry Steele III on May 31, 1984. She and I went to Louisville as soon as we received the news. I was very happy over the name they gave him! I told Bill, "You are smart to call him Berry and avoid name confusion."

Ginny lost another sibling in 1984. Libby died at the age of sixty-three. Breast cancer, thought to have been eliminated, returned and could not be overcome. Both of us had been close to Libby, and we took her passing hard. She experienced much heartbreak in her life but had borne it well. Her daughter, Beth, moved in with Robert and was a big help to him.

In May 1985, Ginny and I took a vacation to Europe with our friends Elsie and David Bickley. They had never been there, and Ginny and I wanted to revisit some of the places we had been in the early 1950s. It was a great trip. We flew into Frankfurt, rented a car, and drove through the southern part of Germany, into Austria, then back through the western side of Germany into France where we explored Paris and Reims. David Bickley enjoyed driving on the German Autobahn with no speed limit while Ginny did not. I took advantage of my retired army status to arrange for us to stay at army VIP facilities along the route.

In the mid-eighties, Aflac was installing a new life insurance computer software program and converting it to suit our supplemental health insurance business. It was a complex, mammoth task and the project had experienced delays. My boss, Kerry Hand, asked me to manage the effort. I did not know much about computer hardware and or software but had experience in managing.

Following that effort, the corporation made some organizational changes and I became director of the conservation, policyholder's service, and payroll accounts departments.

Jack Roland, the real estate agent at Venture Out, called me one day in 1985. He said, "You told me to call you if Mrs. Laidlaw ever wanted to sell Lot 506. Well, she does. Are you still interested in it?"

Without hesitation, I said, "Yes, I will buy it!"

Afterward, I realized I had not even asked for the price. It was a large lot—one of the first sold when Venture Out opened. We sold our current lot and bought a used park model travel trailer for our new lot. Through the years, we made changes and additions resulting in the current beach house.

1985 was also the year in which Bill graduated from the Baptist seminary. Ginny and I attended the ceremony and were extremely proud of the first minister in the Steele, Walton, Berry, or Akin families. His first church assignment was in the small rural community of Springfield, Kentucky. He and Debbie lived in the parsonage next to the church.

They became interested in mission work, applied for the Baptist Foreign Mission Board, and were accepted. After much deliberation, they elected to serve in what was, at the time, Yugoslavia. First, they had to attend a training program for several months in Richmond, Virginia. After that course, they moved to Belgrade, Yugoslavia, where they underwent language and cultural training for three years before assuming their full mission responsibilities there. We were not happy to see them go but knew they had responded to a call from the Lord to do so.

Ginny's mother's health had been failing, and she was in an Augusta nursing home when she died. She was ready to go and had prayed for God to take her. He answered her prayers and she died in her sleep on January 12, 1986, at age ninety-four. She was put to rest next to her husband, Claude, in the Vienna Cemetery. I took Ginny back to Thomson a few months later to meet with her remaining siblings. Ginny's sister, Helen, executed their mother's will. Her estate was small but each heir received a little money and was able to select a few of her personal items for themselves.

The deaths in Ginny's family caused her and her remaining siblings to put more emphasis on family gatherings. Someone held a family reunion nearly every year. Helen and Ginny were the initiators for most of those. In addition, the siblings planned weekends together in Augusta, Atlanta, and Calloway Gardens, Georgia. These were sweet gatherings and provided dear memories for all.

The years 1985–1988 were stable years. For me, supervision of three administrative departments was routine. Ginny was promoted to budget officer for the Infantry School Brigade (where the students were assigned while at Benning) and had an assistant. Therefore, we had more time to play.

The Smithers asked us to join them for a three-week trip to England. We met them in London and shared an apartment for three days while we toured the city. Then we rented a car and spent two wonderful weeks visiting the southern half of England. Sam and I had trouble learning to drive on the wrong side of the road. We stayed in bed & breakfasts and partook of the local dishes. These places were interesting and friendly, particularly in Stratford-upon-Avon, Shakespeare's hometown. The roofs of the houses were thatched, and I wondered how that kept the rain out.

We spent every possible weekend at our beach house in Venture Out. Ginny and I enjoyed the beach and spent lots of time in the sun. Our "someday" had arrived and we were enjoying it. Unfortunately, that time in the sun has since caused me to make numerous visits to dermatologists for treatment of pre-cancerous lesions and the removal of several cancerous areas. (I know, I know. I should have been wearing a hat!)

In November 1987, I became assistant director of U.S. Marketing working for a fine manager, Penny Pennington. I assisted him with national sales strategy and management, as well as supervision of activities in support of the sales effort. The U.S. Marketing Department was certainly a more exciting place to work. The year 1988 started off with a motivational gathering of key sales coordinators in Hong Kong. Ginny went along and helped me mix pleasure with work. We came home laden with purchases we did not need but could not pass up because of the good prices! We had some clothes tailored while we were there and purchased other clothing, jewelry, watches, luggage, leather jackets, wallets, ties, scarves, ivory carvings, and numerous trinkets. But I don't think we really saved any money.

Unlike our army life, Ginny was not as much involved in my work at Aflac. However, she did a lot toward team-building by having my staff and co-workers over for social activities.

1988 was a busy year. I spent a lot of time among the sales force introducing new products and attending meetings. Sometimes I was gone at the wrong time. For example, I was stuck in New Orleans one weekend during a snow storm while Ginny was at home dealing with a broken water pipe that flooded our bedroom. She did not appreciate my long-range support!

Wade began driving again and had another accident. He stepped on the accelerator instead of the brake and drove the car into a convenience store. He lost his license to drive again. His drinking increased and the detoxification process became more difficult. On one occasion, we almost lost him. He was in the hospital for over a week and was in critical condition for two days. Not long after he completed that rehab period, he started drinking again. Ginny and I felt helpless and torn. We were urged by many, including Bill, to exercise tough love and stop enabling him. This was a necessary step, but a hard one for us to take. He was our son.

November 1988 brought further personnel changes at Aflac. I was offered the position of senior vice president for international sales (except for Japan). I had mixed emotions. I felt qualified for the job because of my master's degree in international relations, but the increased traveling would be time-consuming.

Ginny and I discussed my offer. I said, "This is an interesting, exciting opportunity. I feel qualified for it. Also, my age will help as Asians have respect for older people. The Aflac president wants me to take it.

Yet it will mean more travel and time away from home."

"I know," she replied. "And this time you will be traveling the world."

My response was lame. "Well, you can go with me on some of the trips, and you will have the time to do so. We can use my Delta frequent flyer points for your tickets. You will enjoy it."

"You promise?"

"Absolutely," I quickly replied.

"When?"

"In January."

Having made that decision, I began to close out my U.S. marketing responsibilities. I was proud that the Aflac sales objective was going to be met that year. All of marketing had worked hard to make it happen. Part of our sales success was also due to the introduction of new products—an accidental death and disability policy and a supplemental health policy. Aflac's total revenue was 2.3 billion that year. (By this writing—2011—it has exceeded 20.7 billion.)

Ginny and I decided to spend Christmas with Bill and his family. We rendezvoused with them in Garmisch, Germany, in the foothills of the beautiful Alps. We carried too much baggage on that trip. In addition to our two large bags with heavy winter clothing, we carried a large bag filled with Christmas presents, another with a small artificial Christmas tree (complete with lights), and another bag with items requested by Bill's family. To complicate matters, we planned to spend a few days at

Oberammergau—a resort town in Bavaria. We flew into Frankfurt and went to the train station by taxi. From there we traveled by train to Oberammergau, then by taxi to our hotel, all in one long day. We were exhausted, and I was ready to dump half the baggage! However, we kept it all plus items we purchased in Oberammergau (ski jackets and Hummel figurines). We were delighted to reach Garmisch and unload. Later that night, when the tree was decorated and Berry was playing with his presents, I whispered to Ginny, "Sorry about my complaints. This scene makes handling all that baggage worthwhile."

She whispered back, "I knew it would."

Bill and Debbie's wedding, December 19, 1981.

*Brian, age five, and
Marie, age three.*

*Whitewater rafting on the Oconee River
with Bill and Debbie in the early 1980s.*

*With David and Elsie Bickley
touring Paris, 1985.*

*Wade at our house on
Widgeon Drive, 1985.*

William "Berry" Steele III,
one year old.

In Hong Kong for an Aflac trip
sales meeting, January 1988.

Ready to leave on an Aflac trip.

CHAPTER 18

Aflac–International and
the Final Task, 1989–1994

Aflac's first venture outside the United States was Japan. It was a great success. Hoping for similar results elsewhere, Aflac began efforts to sell its products in nine additional countries. Unfortunately, these were not successful. In 1989, Aflac was in Canada, England, Germany, Italy, Korea, Hong Kong, Taiwan, Thailand, and Australia. My mission was to make our sales efforts in these countries successful or consider their closure.

After analyzing our operations in each country, initial decisions were made to close the offices in Germany and Italy due to imposed restrictions by their respective governments. Australia, Taiwan, Hong Kong, Korea, and Thailand required more attention while new approaches were needed in England and Canada. My staff and I started implementing the plan. In the process more and more closures were necessary.

We began by reorganizing the company in England and locating a new manager for it. While there for that purpose, I stayed in an apartment in the Kensington area of London. On one occasion, Ginny stayed with me for several weeks. During the day while I was working, she toured London. One weekend we went by rail to York—a place steeped in English history. On another rainy weekend we went to Edinburgh, Scotland, and saw the palace home of Mary, Queen of Scots. We enjoyed seeing new things—together.

1989 was also the year Ginny began having pain in her lower back and her right hip. In early 1990, she required surgery on her lower back. One night while recuperating, she said, "I am thinking about retiring. I am now sixty-two years old and can retire with either Social Security or civil service benefits."

I replied, "Why not? You have worked long enough. You deserve some time to read, use the computer, and just do what you want. We will be okay financially. Frankly, I will be glad to have you available to travel with me."

"Then I will do it," she replied.

This was a timely decision. Our new granddaughter, Sara Skarpness Steele, was born May 10, 1990, in Vienna, Austria. We went to see Sara, our latest blessing.

Ginny also spent more time with her siblings. Her brother R.C. developed an inoperable, cancerous, brain tumor. After two chemotherapy treatments, he discontinued treatment because of the resulting discomfort. He went home and received hospice care. Ginny drove to Macon frequently to sit with him before he passed away at sixty years old. He was her third sibling to die from cancer, and his death was difficult for her. I wondered who might be next and prayed it would not be Ginny!

Certainly, she seemed destined for difficulties more structural in nature. The pain in her hip began to worsen and walking became increasingly painful. After a trip to Disney World in Orlando with Wade's children (where she took advantage of every available bench), Ginny decided to do something about it. We saw Dr. Savory at the Hughson Orthopedic Clinic in Columbus. He was a retired army colonel, and we quickly related to each other. The tests indicated the need for a hip joint replacement. The surgery was difficult but successful. She worked hard on her post-operative therapy and was soon back in stride.

By this time the work to improve our international sales was well underway in the countries involved. I traveled extensively and when the situation permitted, Ginny accompanied me. She got to know some of the people involved, and we had time to see the sights. I used my Delta frequent flyer points for Ginny's airline tickets.

Closing an insurance company was not easy, especially in another country. I made several trips to Italy trying to expedite matters. Ginny spent some time with me there. She enjoyed window shopping in Rome but managed to buy a beautiful, soft, red, leather, three-quarter-length coat! We saw some of the sights and relaxed at the sidewalk cafes watching the parade of Italian people. We had fun being together in such a romantic place.

One weekend we went by a small boat into the Blue Grotto on the Isle of Capri. The interior of the cave was in shades of blue from the light reflecting off the water. We enjoyed a marvelous lunch at a mountaintop café with a beautiful view. On another short tour, we visited the home of Saint Francis in the town of Assisi.

On the flight back to the United States, I nudged Ginny and said, "Did this trip make up for some of my previous absences?"

She looked back at me with a half-smile and said, "A little."

Korea was another difficult case. The government did not want Aflac to leave, and the worker's organization delayed us at every turn. In the process, I made many trips to Korea trying to extricate us. In the winter of 1992, when my trip there became extended, I asked Ginny to join me. The economy of Seoul was thriving and offered a myriad of products at relatively good prices. Ginny took advantage of it. We also took some time to visit the Demilitarized Zone. It was a vivid reminder of the war I had missed and the reality that there was still just a truce between the two Koreas, not an end to the differences. Unfortunately, Ginny spent the first two days in bed taking anti-inflammatory medicine for neck pain. Arthritis was taking its toll on her.

There was one occasion when I traveled to St. Petersburg, Russia. It was shortly after the dissolution of the Soviet Union, and people were interested in getting capitalistic enterprises started. My purpose was to discuss with some local businessmen things to consider in starting up an insurance company (not for Aflac). I had a chance to see that city after years of communism. The historical sites were interesting but poorly maintained, the newer buildings were already in need of repair, the infrastructure was in need of being updated, and poverty was evident. The Russian airplane I flew was poorly maintained (my seat back would not stay in place). Most of the money had been spent on military muscle during the Cold War.

After attending an international insurance conference in Paris, Ginny and I flew to Bern, Switzerland. Bill met us there, and we drove to Interlaken where he attended a meeting with other European missionaries. It was a beautiful, scenic town nestled between two large lakes. I spent one lazy, sunny afternoon lying on the grass by one of the lakes watching Ginny care for baby Sara while her parents took a twenty-five mile bike ride.

"Ginny. It can't get much better than this."

When she was not traveling with me or enjoying our home and backyard, Ginny was writing a cookbook. She gathered recipes from her family and friends and combined them with favorite recipes of hers to produce a fine cookbook. She had 1,000 copies of *Cook's Pride* printed. She gave copies to friends, kept some for future family members, and sold some to the public.

We continued to enjoy having Brian and Marie visit us frequently on the weekends. Ginny cooked their favorite meals, and they swam in the pool. Sometimes they went with us to Venture Out.

On the way there, Ginny always asked, "What would you two like to eat while we are there?"

Brian would lean his long arms over our seat and shout out, "I want boiled shrimp!"

Marie would chime in, "Lasagna is what I want."

Ginny would usually prepare both. Brian and Marie were growing up too quickly. We felt blessed to have them close by and to spend so much time with them. They were good children.

Wade was still with Kathan in spite of periodic bouts with his addiction.

To her credit, she was dealing with it without any help from me. She also took advantage of local agencies available to help dry out and rehabilitate alcoholics.

I thought he might overcome his addiction when he resided with the Valley Rescue Mission for nine months. He lived at their farm facility and worked at their store for several months. The farm had about six to eight residents and a strong senior resident to keep them in line. Wade respected him and seemed to be doing well. Ginny and I periodically took Brian and Marie to see him and maintain contact with their father. It also gave Wade some support and motivation.

When Wade completed his stay at the farm, we invited him to go to the beach house with us for a weekend. While we were at the beach one afternoon, Wade went back to the house to get something. When he did not return in a reasonable time, we went to check on him. We found him on his bed, passed out. We could not understand where he got something to drink because I had removed all the liquor. When he woke up, he was still intoxicated. The next day he told us he had found a bottle of rubbing alcohol under the bathroom sink and drank it all. This was a sad time for us.

In 1993 Bill was still living in Belgrade, Serbia, but had assumed responsibility for administering the Baptist mission effort in a number of additional Balkan countries—Slovenia, Croatia, Kosovo, Bosnia, Macedonia, Albania, Bulgaria, and Greece. The mission also coordinated the reception, travel arrangements, logistical support, and problem solving for the incoming missionaries and volunteer groups. Debbie was a big help where family counseling was needed and in working with local start-up churches.

Travel across the Serbian border was difficult and dangerous due to the growing conflict between Serbia and the other former Yugoslavian countries. He moved his family to Ljubljana, Slovenia, in June 1993. It was also a safer environment for the children. They went to local schools and learned to speak Slovenian. Berry had already learned Serbo-Croatian. Debbie also homeschooled them.

We spent Christmas with them in 1993. (This time they provided the Christmas tree.) It snowed on Christmas Eve, and Bill and I helped Berry build a snowman and participated in a snowball fight with him and his friends. Bill and Debbie prepared Christmas dinner. Ginny enjoyed watching and I enjoyed eating!

Ginny's sister, Helen, died that year, at sixty-eight years old. She had a mole on her back which went untreated and developed into melanoma. She did not have long from the time of its discovery until her death. She spent most of that time undergoing chemotherapy in an Augusta hospital. I took Ginny there and stayed a few days before returning to work. I knew from the look Helen gave me when we said goodbye that she knew we would not see each other again. Ginny and her brother Johnny were the last ones left in the family. He was ten years older than Ginny, and I thought he would probably be the next to leave this earth. I was wrong.

The loss of Ginny's siblings and her worsening arthritic condition made me seriously think about retirement from Aflac. We needed more time together to do the things we wanted to do before her mobility became restricted. We had talked about extended visits to the beach house and seeing the states in a motor home, going and stopping as we pleased.

I contacted Aflac President Dan Amos. "I would like to retire in August of 1994 when I become sixty-five years old."

As I recall, he said, "Okay, your assistant, Ralph Illges, can take over from you later this year. You can wind down by doing some special projects for me until August 1994."

I really appreciated his consideration, glad that I would not have to experience the abrupt change in pace I experienced when I retired from the Army. Aflac was extremely fortunate to have Dan leading the corporation.

I knew Ralph could handle my job. He was a smart, personable young man with a law degree. He was also good with numbers. He gained some experience filling in for me that winter while I was in Toronto managing the Canadian branch and looking for a new manager.

Ginny came with me for several days. She loved snow, and we had plenty of it.

When my time with international ended in late summer, only two companies remained—Canada and Taiwan. (They have since been closed.) Although unfortunate, I believe these were correct business actions and handled in the best way possible.

The 1993 Aflac Convention in the fall was the last one that Ginny and I attended. We would miss these gatherings and the distinguished speakers that attended. To me, the most impressive speaker I met was former President Ronald Reagan.

My final mission at Aflac before retirement was to form a small research group and determine what Aflac should look like twenty years in the future. A lot of research, analysis, and computer modeling was needed, along with sharp, inquisitive minds. With executive support, I was able to gather a few people, and we began.

As soon as I was comfortable with our progress, I reduced my office time. Aflac was an outstanding example of American enterprise, and caring management; it had been a wonderful, rewarding experience, but retirement was beginning to look better and better.

Elsie Bickley and Elizabeth Lewis in the early 1990s.

Attending an international insurance conference, Paris.

With former President Ronald Reagan at an Aflac convention.

Berry (six years old) and Sara Skarpness Steele (one year old).

CHAPTER 19
Retirement: 1994–2000

In August 1994 following my retirement from Aflac, Ginny and I were very happy. We looked forward to the next phase of our life together with great anticipation. We were free to do whatever we desired and had the financial security to do so.

We had seen a lot of the world but wanted to enjoy the many interesting, beautiful places in the United States. We wanted to do so while we were still healthy enough to travel. We purchased a twenty-nine-foot Winnebago that could sleep six people (if they were related to each other or were close friends). It would be great for the two of us.

We divided our time between being at home for local events, staying at the beach house, and traveling in the RV. We planned our time each year, leaving flexibility for unforeseen circumstances. Unfortunately, those unforeseen circumstances began to occur more frequently than anticipated.

First, we saw a house for sale that we liked in the Copper Oaks subdivision. For some time, Ginny had wanted to relocate. She wanted a house that had more openness between the kitchen, dining, and living areas. She said I needed a smaller yard to maintain.

The minute we walked inside the house, we both knew it was the one for us. I heard Ginny gasp, "Look at the openness between the kitchen, the breakfast area, and the den! Why, there are windows all across the rear so you can see the backyard from any part of the house! I love the floor plan."

I agreed. "The layout is just the way we wanted it plus the yard is small."

She quickly added, "But the colors are all wrong. The walls will need repainting and we need different color carpeting."

I knew the desired response. "Well . . . that can be done."

Three hours later, we made an offer and by early afternoon, signed a sales contract with a move-in date of May 1995.

Another unforeseen circumstance occurred when Ginny woke one night with severe stomach pain. We went to the St. Francis Hospital emergency room, and she was diagnosed with appendicitis. She was admitted that night and operated on the next morning. Her appendix had been on the verge of rupturing.

Our poodle, Cece, died of heart failure after a nighttime seizure. A quick trip to the animal clinic and efforts to revive her failed. We buried her in the backyard next to Ginny's favorite poodle, Pepe. He had drowned less than a year earlier. He fell into the pool one evening and got sucked into the pool skimmer. Apparently, his eyesight had deteriorated, and he lost his way. We buried him in the backyard that night in the rain. Ginny rained tears for a long time afterward. We decided not to have any more pets; losing them brought too much sorrow.

A few days before our yard sale and the moving date, Ginny suffered stomach pains again and required emergency gall bladder surgery. It was done arthroscopically, which was not as invasive as regular surgery. Her recovery was quick. But during the yard sale and our move, she had to watch from the sidelines. Fortunately, Elizabeth and Marie were there to assist. Finally, Ginny was able to rest during a move.

1995 through 1999 were wonderful years. We traveled in our RV, spent more time at the beach, and visited Bill and his family in Europe.

In June 1995 Bill and his family came to the United States on a six-month furlough, so that he could work on his doctorate at the Baptist seminary in Louisville. We invited them to join us on a trip to Colorado, Montana, Wyoming, and South Dakota. We were limited by the time they had, and RV camping sites were crowded in the summer. The trip was planned and reservations were made well in advance. We adhered to a strict schedule. I was accustomed to this but the rest of the group had some trouble with my "rather inflexible schedule."

While we all rode in the motor home and pulled our car behind it for use on side trips, I was concerned about the crowded sleeping arrangements. We booked cabins for Bill's family at each of the scheduled stops. In retrospect, I should have opted for more togetherness.

Ginny and I enjoyed spending quality time with the family. We traveled about 5,000 miles and spent time at Jackson Hole, Wyoming, explored Yellowstone National Park, walked the ground where Custer

made his last stand, toured the Badlands, and saw the presidential moun-
tainside sculptures.

The next spring, Ginny and I decided to travel north along the east
coast and into Canada without a schedule. We had a marvelous time.
We spent several days in Fredericksburg, Virginia, visiting Civil War
battle sites. We revisited the Carlisle area and enjoyed the Amish area.
We spent a few days in Newport, Rhode Island, and stopped by the scene
of Woodstock. We visited Roosevelt's former home in New York, blew
through Massachusetts, Vermont, and New Hampshire, then drove
along the coastline of Maine, stopping whenever the mood struck us.
(We ate many lobsters.) We stopped by President Bush's home at Ken-
nebunkport but decided not to call on him. We left our motor home at a
RV camp in northern Maine, and drove the car to New Brunswick and
Prince Edward Island, and took the ferry to Nova Scotia. We were gone
for almost a month and, as always, were happy to return to our nest.

On several occasions, we met Don and Doris Carmean (our friends
from Venture Out) at various locations. They were also avid RV travelers.

We spent time with them during March each year at Key West, or on
Chokoloskee Island, Florida. Chokoloskee Island was a quiet, relaxing,
quaint place with a world-class RV resort. We ate, read, exercised, swam,
sunned, and slept.

One year, we met Don and a friend at the Grand Canyon. They had
a tradition of walking the Grand Canyon every year. They prided them-

selves on still being able to do that with Don in his 70s and his friend in his 80s.

Our last long trip was in early spring of 2000. Ginny read about the Grand Hotel on Mackinac Island at Lake Michigan. We spent a few days in the area. The hotel was a large, beautiful, white, wooden structure with a big front porch. It was a picturesque sight nestled in a wooded area with a beautiful, expansive, sloping lawn. We enjoyed a leisurely lunch, feeling as though we were back at the end of the nineteenth century.

We then traveled westward to see the Arneckes in San Antonio. A few days later we headed back to the east coast. Stopping in Lafayette, Louisiana, to enjoy some Cajun cooking, we bought a new thirty-seven-foot Damon Motor Home. (I talked about getting a larger motor home for a while since I was concerned about Ginny's ability to get in and out of one as her arthritis worsened. We needed a lift for a wheelchair and enough space for the wheelchair to maneuver in.)

On the way back to Columbus in our new RV, we stopped in Ponchatoula, Louisiana, to see Bill and his family. (They had moved there in January 2000 after returning from the Balkan countries.) Bill and Debbie realized Berry would do better in college if he finished high school in a U.S. school. Ginny and I were glad to have them back in the states. Debbie also wanted to return to school and pursue a master's degree in marriage and family counseling at the Baptist seminary in New Orleans. Ponchatoula was nearby, and a house was available there for use by a missionary on sabbatical at no cost. Bill supported Debbie's goal. She had taken courses toward her masters while Bill was working on his doctorate in Louisville. Now she could finish in New Orleans. Bill assumed the responsibility of caring for the children and the household.

We continued to enjoy Wade's children, too. We had some fun trips to the beach, Washington, D.C., and Disney World. They enjoyed traveling by plane for the first time as well as seeing where some of the history of the United States occurred.

By 2000, both Brian and Marie were out of high school. Brian was working and Marie started college. Brenda had married Andrew Ellis, a good man who was kind to Brian and Marie. They moved into Andrew's house in a nice area of Phenix City.

Unfortunately, Kathan and her children no longer wanted Wade in their lives. He was living in one room of an old building where several other homeless men lived. In the summer of 1999 Wade became very ill with a respiratory problem. He was diagnosed with bronchitis, but upon further evaluation, a suspicious spot was detected on his lung. He was moved to the University of Georgia's Doctors Hospital in Augusta where a biopsy was taken. Ginny and I went to Augusta to be with him. We had passed the point of tough love. The biopsy indicated cancer, and an operation was needed to remove a portion of his left lung.

During surgery, it was necessary to remove his left lung. He stayed there for several days and was released to recover at home.

Kathan volunteered to move in with him and provide care during his recovery. I provided food and financial support. After three months, he was well enough for light work. But to occupy his mind and give him more recuperative time, I enrolled him in some computer classes at Columbus Vocational Technical School.

About two months later, a doctor from the university hospital called and asked for Wade to attend a meeting concerning his case. I was invited to attend. The doctor acknowledged that Wade's biopsy had gotten switched with another person's biopsy. Wade's biopsy had not been cancerous.

Instead of operating, they should have watched Wade's lung to see if cancer developed. They did point out that during the surgery, they found Wade's lung condition so bad that removal of one side was still needed. However, the news was a blow to all of us and very depressing.

We hired a local attorney to take Wade as a client on a percentage basis. He initiated a damage suit on Wade's behalf. This was settled by arbitration and took a long time to complete. Simultaneously, we initiated action to get Wade on disability. This too moved at a snail's pace.

I continued to provide financial support with the stipulation Wade was not to drink or smoke. When I found him talking with some other men with a can of beer in one hand and a cigarette in the other, I ended all support.

Wade died November 2, 2000. He was working at a Columbus lumber yard and living in a trailer owned by a co-worker near Cusseta, Georgia. When the co-worker did not see him one morning, he checked and found that Wade had died sitting in a chair. I got there just as the ambulance arrived, but I could not bring myself to go in and see him. I did not want to carry that memory of him with me the rest of my life.

We arranged for Wade to be taken to Vienna for the funeral and burial in the family plot at the Lilly Cemetery. Bill spoke at the graveside service. His remarks reflected his love for his brother and the reality that no one knew what demons Wade had to battle during his addiction. To this day, I wonder what I could have done to cause Wade's life to have been different. Somehow, I should have helped him develop more self-confidence. I am heartened, however, when I remember that his life was not without purpose. He helped give birth to two wonderful human beings—Brian and Marie.

Had he lived another year, he would have been able to see Brian get married. Brian and Angela "Angie" Brooke Davis were married on August 4, 2001. Angie was one of Marie's high school classmates—a sweet, blue-eyed girl with a pretty face. They had a beautiful church wedding and spent their honeymoon at the beach house. Brian and Angie purchased a trailer and began their life together in Smith's Station, Alabama. She was attending Chattahoochee Valley Community College at the time, and Brian was working at an auto servicing facility in Phenix City.

Sadly, while Wade was going through his illness, Ginny's health was deteriorating.

The grandchildren: Brian, Marie,
Sara, and Berry in the early 1990s.

Visiting with Bill and his
family in Slovenia, 1994.

Visiting with Bill and his
family in Germany, 1995.

Motor home trip out west with Bill and his family, 1995.

Bill receives his doctorate, 1996.

Ginny 1996.

*High school senior, Brian,
1998.*

*High school senior, Marie,
2000.*

Brian marries Angela Brooke Davis, August 4, 2001.

CHAPTER 20
Ginny: 2000–2003

Ginny began to have pain in her knee and we went back to Dr. Savory. He replaced her knee joint. The surgery was successful, but she continued to have pain. We spent Christmas (complete with turkey and dressing) in our new motor home in the Daytona Beach area.

Ginny's lower back began hurting again, and we consulted with Dr. Adams. Fusion of four or five vertebra was required. He considered it too risky because of her age and physical condition. When the pain worsened, Dr. Adams agreed to remove a single offending piece of bone. She recovered and went without severe pain for a while, but her lower back problem persisted.

We went to the Emory Clinic in Atlanta in September 2001. Dr. Brian Suback could operate and fuse five vertebras. Ginny wanted to wait until after Christmas, so we set the surgery for January. We were upbeat on the way back to Columbus.

I said, "Ginny, he seemed very positive didn't he?"

"Yes," she replied. "He is an impressive person. I feel confident with him doing the surgery."

In December 2001, Dr. Suback developed a medical problem which prevented him from operating until March 28. Ginny wanted to wait. This was a mistake. Her mobility decreased and her overall health deteriorated rapidly over the next few months.

Bill drove to Atlanta and joined us the night before her surgery. I was glad to see him. His support was welcome. I was worried over Ginny's condition, sad about her pain, and concerned about the upcoming operation.

The operation lasted for six long hours. It was deemed successful, but she was in recovery for three hours. She spent five days in the hospital and I slept in the room with her. When she did not respond fast enough to the physical therapy, she was moved to the Emory rehab facility for a slower rehab program. I moved into a nearby hotel. She still did not progress fast enough and needed to be moved to another, more long-term, facility. At this point, we decided to find one in Columbus.

On April 15 she went to the rehabilitation section of the Hamilton House nursing home, in Columbus. On May 15 four weeks later, she was released to continue her rehab at home. We were so happy but celebrated too soon.

The first night at home, she was feverish and racked with back pain. I decided to take her back to Emory. I know she could feel every bump in the road but each time I asked, "How are you doing?" she responded, "I am okay."

She was a strong person. After we arrived she was moved from lab to lab, undergoing tests all afternoon. I could see the pain and misery in her eyes, but she tried to be cheerful and managed to say thank you to everyone who worked on her case. She was diagnosed with a staph infection in the area of her operation and was admitted to Emory Hospital later that day. She was operated on the following morning to clean out the affected area. Fortunately, the infection had not spread into the bone. She had to undergo weeks of intravenously administrated antibiotics back in Hamilton House.

On July 17 she came back home again and I was hopeful for her continued recovery. She started out-patient physical therapy at St. Francis' Health Dynamics Center. Her progress was slow, and we did not see any progress for months. She tried very hard, but her muscles didn't strengthen. She endured pain without complaint and took setbacks with grace and patience. She was always a good trooper.

In January 2003 Ginny realized she was not going to get better and wanted to go to Venture Out one more time. We did not usually go in the winter but we did that year. She was using a wheelchair, and I had installed a monorail lift for her to go up and down the stairs. Getting around was still difficult.

In March 2003 the physical therapist and I agreed that Ginny was regressing, rather than progressing.

We still had hope and began seeing a glandular specialist, Dr. Leichter. Ginny had a long history of an under-active thyroid gland and a recent history of diabetes. He did a series of blood tests that indicated her adrenal and pituitary glands were not functioning properly. She was no longer growing muscle. He prescribed a new medicine designed to promote muscle growth. However, it would take six months or more to begin showing results.

I had begun to use a home health care service periodically to give me time to do other necessary things. As time went on, I used them more frequently. Some of them were very helpful; others just wanted to sit and watch television.

Ginny taught me how to cook, one meal at a time. She told me what to do, and I would follow orders. Our biggest problem was choosing food within her diabetic restrictions. She was innovative, especially when it pertained to food.

I might offer, "Ginny, how about some baked salmon tonight?"

She responded, "Okay but why don't you fix a nice sauce to put on it? I will tell you how to make it. First you need some dill, some olive oil . . ."

By the time I finished, we had a tasty dish—thanks to her.

Marie's wedding was scheduled for June 28, 2003. Ginny was in a wheelchair, and I was really pleased that she was able to be at the wedding. Marie married Brandon Culpepper, a high school classmate. They were a nice-looking couple. Marie was beautiful in a long, white dress, and Brandon looked sharp in his tux. He was working in Opelika as an automotive technician, and Marie had a job with a bank in nearby Auburn.

By then, Ginny was using a hospital-style bed. I had one put in the bedroom along with a twin bed for my use. Somehow, I kept thinking she would get better and, even though she could not walk, we would still be together. Her mind was still sharp.

On August 2, 2003, after a weekend in which she ate very little because of a throat irritation called thrush, she became extremely listless. I called an ambulance, and she was taken to St. Francis Hospital and a feeding tube was inserted to provide nourishment.

Although this was less intrusive than her other surgeries, she never fully recovered from it. I suppose it was one blow too many for her system. After several days of treatment with no response, I was faced with a decision regarding further life support measures. She and I had discussed this and made our living wills accordingly. I knew what she wanted but had a hard time coming to grips with that decision. I called Bill and talked with him. Then I told the doctor to stop everything, including water.

I spent the next ten days watching her die. It was the worst experience of my life. I was with her and held her when she took her last breath at 4:30 p.m. on August 21, 2003—four days after our 54th wedding anniversary.

Fortunately, Bill arrived a few days before Ginny died. He was supportive and helped with the funeral arrangements. We both had a hard time getting through the service which was held, at her request, at the Vienna Baptist Church. The service was attended by many of her local friends in addition to some who traveled from Columbus. She was then buried at the Lilly Cemetery.

The immediate family gathered at our (my) house later that day, and I gave them the jewelry and other personal items that Ginny wanted them to have. After Bill left, the enormity of her absence hit me.

A range of emotions went through me: shock, disbelief, denial, anger, guilt, and depression. I did everything possible to stay busy and not think about her death. I removed everything that reminded me of her suffering from the house. This did not ease my pain.

The ensuing months were spent trying to adjust to life without Ginny; they were difficult. Ginny and I had been close to three couples for many years—the Bickleys, the Thompsons, and the Walkers. They tried their best to help me through this difficult period. I continued to be included in the periodic couples' dinners, but I was no longer a couple without Ginny. Things weren't the same for me.

In the fall, I went on a cruise and then spent a few days before Christmas with Bill and his family in Hammond, Louisiana. (They had purchased a house there after a year in Ponchatoula.)

Something was needed to bring me out of my sadness. Nothing I did seemed meaningful, and the pain of Ginny's death was constantly in my thoughts. One morning I woke up with the realization that I could not fix things by myself. I needed help—God's help.

While I considered myself a Christian, I had not grown spiritually, nor did I have a close, personal relationship with God. I realized then, that I needed to take God into my heart—turn my life over to Him, look to Him for direction, and have complete faith in Him; I needed to affiliate myself with a church. God led me to Wynnbrook Baptist Church. Although it was a short distance from where I lived, it was a large step for me that led to a big change in my life.

From the beginning, I was comfortable at Wynnbrook. The pastor, Dr. Brad Hicks, visited me. We had a long conversation where I was relaxed and expressed myself freely. He was a teaching pastor, one I could respect and learn from. The church members were warm in their welcome, the Sunday school class included some retired military folks I knew, and several bible study groups were available.

I participated in guest services work and helped develop long-range plans for growth of the church. In October someone nominated me to become a deacon. I declined, not feeling spiritually mature enough for any position of leadership. However, after some urging, I agreed to serve in that role. When I told Bill, he suggested that I might regret getting involved in church leadership because of the personality conflicts that often develop. I saw some of this, but as the result of my closer relationship with God and my involvement in church activities, my outlook on life improved considerably.

My improved demeanor gave some the idea that I might be ready for female companionship. Several people approached me about meeting one of his or her female friends. At that point in time, I did not visualize myself developing a relationship with another woman—certainly not at my age! Finally, in late May 2004, I agreed to three of those most persistent. Lunch meetings were subsequently arranged, but they simply confirmed my earlier misgivings about another woman being in my life. God, however, had other plans.

Marie marries Brandon Culpepper, June 28, 2004.

CHAPTER 21
Sandy: Another Love, 2004–2005

On June 10, 2004, God's plan began to unfold. I had attended a committee meeting at the church and went to my branch bank in the Bradley Park shopping area to cash a check. As I was leaving the bank, a woman stopped me. She was striking—trim, about five feet four inches tall, blond hair, and pretty blue eyes. I was taken aback and didn't recognize her, although she looked familiar.

She said, "I know you. Bill Steele! Your wife and my mother shared a room for a short time at the Hamilton House."

"I'm sorry," I apologized. "I don't recall your name."

"Sandy. Sandy Cross. We talked on several occasions when we were visiting at the same time."

At that point, I put it all together and remembered.

She continued, "I saw Ginny's obituary in the newspaper. How are you getting along?"

"I am doing okay," I replied. "It has been a very difficult year but I know that it is time to get on with my life."

"I am sure it has been difficult for you," she said. It was obvious that you loved her very much."

"Very," I replied. "How have you been? How is your mother?"

"She had more surgery and is currently bedridden and living with me."

Recalling that she was married, I asked, "How about your husband?"

She replied, "We are separated. We were separated when he was with me at the rehab center. He's been having a long-time affair with another woman."

I was very surprised. When they were visiting her mother together, she had introduced him as her husband.

We exchanged a few pleasantries and parted company; she remained to see a bank officer and I went home.

While driving home, I thought about how cheerful and pleasant she was in the hospital room despite the suffering. I recalled the kind, loving way she cared for her mother and how easy it was to converse with her, then and now. I felt comfortable with her. Perhaps we could become friends. Perhaps we could get together for lunch or other outings. Perhaps I should call her. Perhaps it really was time to get on with my life!

Some advice I received after Ginny's death came to mind. Arthur Morgan, another country boy and friend from my days at Vienna High, wrote to me about how he had lost his wife and suffered greatly. Yet, he had met another wonderful woman and was able to love again, remarry, and be happy. He encouraged me to be open to the possibility.

There were still more reservations. I did not know her age but I was certainly older—too old for her? Was she still hoping to reconcile with her husband? What if she just said "No"? Could I deal with rejection? Was I ready to take this step? The drive home took only eight minutes but, by the time I got there, the decision was made. *Call her!*

How was I to find her telephone number? There wasn't a Sandy Cross listed in the telephone book, but there were several listings for the name Cross. I started dialing. Fortunately, her grandson Bradley answered the first number I called. He gave me a number where she could be reached. The number was listed in her husband's name. No one answered, so I left a message.

She did not return my call. Not to be discouraged, I called again and learned that she had returned the first call. I had forgotten that the initial call was made on the alternate phone line for my computer. (I didn't check for messages on that phone.) She agreed to my luncheon invitation without hesitation though we didn't set a date yet. She had a girlfriend visiting for a few days, and I was going to a reunion of my Vietnam unit in Dallas the following week.

She showed no urgency and said to call her after I returned. I was ready to firm up a lunch date immediately, as is my nature, but did not want to seem anxious.

The reunion of the former members of the 5th Battalion (Mechanized), 60th Infantry was both heartwarming and sad. Seeing and talking with so many men who had served with me in Vietnam and meeting their wives was a real joy. We shared our recollection of events and the people we had known, as well as information about what we had done since. We all felt sorrow, remembering those who were killed or severely wounded. In view of the outcome of the war, we felt our losses were all for nothing.

They gave me an opportunity to address the group after dinner one night. I reviewed some of our battles, praised the members for their courage, and thanked them for their service. During the entire weekend, they made me feel welcome and many expressed their gratitude for my leadership. I must admit this was heartening to me. I wished Ginny was by my side. She had shared all of my troop assignments except this one, and she would have welcomed the opportunity to meet some of those fine soldiers.

This was only one of many times I missed her. She had been a part of my life for fifty-four years. How would she feel about my meeting Sandy? She would probably have mixed feelings. I know I would, if the reverse was true. I would be sad that someone else might be in her life but happy that she wasn't alone for the remainder of her life. I prayed Ginny felt that way about me.

Although there was a slight twinge of guilt about asking a woman to join me for lunch, I approached my impending lunch meeting with youthful anticipation. For the first time in a long time, I was excited about something and really looked forward to the event.

I wanted the luncheon arrangements to facilitate our getting to know each other. We needed an upscale, quiet, relaxing environment. Unfortunately, because of her mother's caretaking needs, Mondays were the only days we could meet. My first choice, the Green Island Club, was closed on Mondays. After some research and on-site inspections, I chose B. Merrill's. It had a varied menu, was easy for her to get to, reconnaissance proved it was quiet, and it had some comfortable booths.

The day finally arrived—July 19. After much deliberation on what to wear, I arrived at the restaurant early and staked out a booth near the window. I could see her when she arrived and meet her at the door.

I suddenly realized that I was nervous, as though this was my first date—correction—meeting. I learned later that she had also been nervous.

After she arrived, I said, "I want to apologize again for not recognizing you at the bank. Perhaps I would have, if I had a moment to think about where I had seen you before."

She replied, "Don't be concerned. I realize that I surprised you when I spoke to you."

I continued. "It was very thoughtful of you to speak to me. We were both going through a sorrowful time with our loved ones in rehab. I appreciate you joining me for lunch. I'd like to get to know you better. Please, tell me about yourself and your life."

"There is not much to tell," she said. "I was born in 1940 in this area and spent all of my childhood in Columbus, in the same house and same school. My father was in the Navy during World War II and later became addicted to alcohol. But I had a strong, caring mother. She was an executive secretary for the local office of the Monroe Calculating Machine Company and taught piano lessons at night to make ends meet. I was also blessed with a loving, sensitive, older brother whom I adored. He died in 2002 and I still miss him."

At this point, I interrupted her. "I am so sorry. Losing a sibling is difficult, especially when you have been close. I heard your description of your childhood with envy. Unlike you, I grew up in a number of towns and went to a lot of different schools. But forgive my interruption. Please continue."

She resumed, "I went to LaGrange College for one year but left when I was eighteen to elope with my high school sweetheart, Jimmy Cross. We had four children. He was in banking and we lived in Columbus and Phenix City, except for short stays in Fort Valley, Georgia, and Hartsell, Alabama."

Again I interrupted. "Is he still in banking?"

"No," she responded. "He is medically retired. He has a heart condition."

"Go on," I prompted. "Tell me about your children."

"My oldest son, Brad, lives in Phenix City with his wife, Elisa, and their sons, Bradley and Brooks. My daughter, Leslie, is living in Athens with her husband Dr. David Suarez, a son named Samuel, and the twins, Thomas and Katharine. My middle son, Kevin, is not married and lives in Columbus. My youngest son, David, lives in Atlanta, with his wife, Megan."

I interjected. "Well it is good that you have family nearby in case you need help."

"Yes," she said. "My husband and I separated several years ago, but he will still help if I need him. Yet, I try not to call on any of them unless it is absolutely necessary. Now, tell me about yourself, Bill. I really know little about you. I didn't know you were military until I looked in the telephone book and saw you were a retired major general."

I gave her a similar brief review of my life, as we sparingly ate our salads. The conversation flowed easily. Before I knew it, two hours had passed and Sandy had to go back home to be with her mother.

While walking her to her car, I told her, "I really enjoyed our lunch. Perhaps we can do this again."

She said, "Sure. I liked it also. But with the differences in our backgrounds, I'm surprised that you would enjoy my company."

"On the contrary," I responded. "The world you know is the world in which I am currently living."

I felt upbeat. It had been a good experience, and I was comfortable with her. Despite the age difference, we had similar likes and dislikes and the same values. She was charming, pleasant, and sensitive—a real southern lady, who was also very attractive. I think Ginny would have liked her.

Several days passed before I saw Sandy again. However, we had some long telephone conversations initiated mostly by me. We learned a lot more about each other.

One day while lunching at the Yogurt Shop, (a good place to lunch), I saw Sandy sitting at a table with an attractive, dark-haired woman.

"Come join us," Sandy invited. "I want you to meet my friend Sally Posey."

After the introductions, she continued, "Sally is seeing former U.S. Congressman Jack Brinkley."

I had met Jack in the early 70s when he represented Georgia's 3d Congressional District in the U.S. House of Representatives. As a member of the House Armed Services Committee, he visited my brigade at Fort Benning to see how the all-volunteer Army was doing. Jack was known as a man of great character and integrity.

Sally suggested, "Let's get together soon."

We did and a close, dear friendship was created among all four of us.

Over the next few months, I thought about my relationship with Sandy and how it might develop into more than just companionship.

By November I was sure I wanted our relationship to progress. Sandy and I went to Atlanta so that I could meet some dear friends of Sandy's—Carole Hollingsworth and Larry Sheber. Carole had been at the bank the day Sandy and I talked. She accurately predicted that I had been "smitten" and would contact Sandy.

It was clear to me that, if I were to have a close relationship with Sandy, I had to be approved by Carole and Larry. He had been friends with Carole for many years and knew Sandy well. Both of them were protective of Sandy. I tried not to say the wrong thing or spill something during lunch but was not sure that I had met expectations.

On the way back to Columbus, I told Sandy, "I don't know if I passed inspection or not. What do you think?"

"Oh yes," she said. "When you went to the restroom, Carole told me she liked you. Larry agreed with her and commented that you were much nicer than the generals he had seen while he was in the Army."

I chuckled and responded, "That's good. In some ways that was more stressful than some army inspections I have undergone."

Then I relaxed and enjoyed the ride. I felt very comfortable with her beside me and realized that I was falling in love.

How would my relationship impact my family, especially Bill? When I first met Sandy, I called Bill and told him. Now I needed to let him know that a relationship was developing.

I called him that evening and after the usual conversation, I said, "Bill, Sandy and I are getting along well, and I am enjoying her company. I believe that our relationship is growing, and I wanted you to know."

"I thought that might happen. Are you sure about this?"

"Yes," I said, "I miss your mother greatly, and no one will ever replace her in my heart. But life without companionship is very lonely. I hope you can understand that." I sensed disappointment on his part but understood his feelings about another woman in my life."

This was less of a problem for my grandchildren. Brian and Marie met Sandy early on and, although somewhat surprised, warmed to Sandy quickly. They saw how much happier I was with Sandy and told me so.

Bill's wife Debbie came to Columbus in the fall to visit her childhood friend, Mary Sparks. Sandy and I joined them for lunch one day. It was a delightful occasion, and Debbie and Sandy seemed very comfortable with each other.

Bill told me in a later telephone conversation, "Debbie said that Sandy was very nice and that she has very pretty eyes."

My sentiments exactly!

Bill and his family came home for the Skarpness family gathering during Thanksgiving. Recognizing it would be a short visit, I still wanted Bill and Sandy to get acquainted. I managed to get everyone together for Thanksgiving lunch at the Green Island Club. Sandy had a bad cold, but knew its importance to me and came, in spite of not feeling well. I expected this to be difficult for Bill. The impact of seeing another woman in my life was bound to be hard for him to accept.

He called me when he returned to Fresno. (Bill had applied for and accepted a position as Director of Ministries for a large non-denominational church in Fresno, California.)

He said, "Dad I just had to call you. I have trouble seeing you alongside someone else besides Mom. It just hurts."

I quickly responded. "I know, I know. I thought you would. It is only natural. I had similar feelings initially. I just ask that you give it time and try to understand my situation. I need someone to be with, to share my life with."

"Yes, that is what Debbie has been telling me. Maybe time will help."

I prayed that would be the case.

While no one would ever replace Ginny, I could love again and live my remaining years in a happier, more meaningful way. Sandy respected Ginny's memory in our hearts and could be a dear friend to Bill.

Sandy's situation was somewhat different. Although she and Jimmy were separated, in the eyes of her children they were still husband and wife. She chose not to tell them about me.

Frequently, we got together with Sally and Jack at Sally's house or we all went somewhere together. The four of us spent Christmas and New Year's Day together, and our friendship grew. Sandy and I became closer and more comfortable together. In addition, Sally and Jack became like a sister and brother to us. It was (and still is) a sweet relationship for the four of us.

A retired army friend of mine saw us in a restaurant one day and came over to speak. I introduced him to Sandy. The next time I saw him he mentioned the occasion and said, "Bill, I thought about seeing you with that young blond the other day. You may be getting in over your head."

I retorted, "You may be right."

I was seventy-five years old but did not feel that age. I planned on living a while longer—a long while. Routinely, I worked out at the Green

Island Country Club fitness room, maintained a healthy diet, and was in good physical condition for my age. My irregular heartbeat was being controlled by a pacemaker. As a result, I felt good and had lots of energy.

In the fall of 2003, Berry had dropped out of college and joined the Armor Branch of the U.S. Army. Although I was disappointed he didn't stay in college (or choose the Infantry), I took solace that there was another soldier in the family.

The day he graduated from training—March 5, 2004— I was especially proud. He made a good-looking trooper. His other grandfather, Norman, and I attended, along with Bill, Debbie, and Sara. We all stayed in the VIP Quarters at Fort Knox and were treated royally. Berry asked me to wear my uniform for the occasion. I was reluctant to do so but did. Fortunately, it still fit, except that the trousers had to be shortened. I had shrunk almost two inches since they were last worn in 1978.

Berry was in great physical shape and was an impressive-looking soldier. I said to Norman, "We both know what he had to do to graduate. I am proud of him."

"Me too. I agree," he responded. "Berry has worked hard, endured things he did not know he could, and has gotten into great physical condition."

"Yes," I added. "He has also learned to obey orders. Maybe before he finishes his tour of service, he will get to a pay grade where he can give some orders."

Unfortunately, I had made things harder for Berry. Shortly after our arrival he told me, "Granddaddy, you caused me to do a lot of extra push-ups."

"How did I do that?"

He responded, "When you let the people at post headquarters know that you were coming, someone told my company first sergeant that retired Major General Steele was attending the company's graduation ceremony. The first sergeant told my drill sergeant. He called me in and said, 'Why didn't you tell me your grandfather was a retired major general?' I told him, 'I didn't know I was supposed to.' He then said, 'You should have known. Give me twenty-five push-ups.'"

Norman rode with me to and from Fort Knox, and we had an opportunity to swap a few war stories. It was a memorable weekend.

After his training at Fort Knox, Berry was assigned to the 3d Mechanized Infantry Brigade at Fort Benning. The brigade was scheduled to deploy to Iraq in January 2005. I spent some time with him before he left. He was using my house as his home away from home. Before he arrived, I bought him a used 1989 Honda sedan. Unfortunately, when he saw it, he wanted something sportier. He bought a 2002 Honda Civic. I loaned him some money for the down payment. (Fortunately, I was able to return the 1989 Honda.)

Initially, I spent some time with him but training and his social life soon took over. He also traded the Civic for an older, more expensive, well-abused, Honda sports model.

When he departed for Iraq in early January, he left his car in my garage, his clothes in my closet, and his electronic toys in my attic. We communicated with Berry via cell phones and emails. He spent a lot of time in field positions and on patrols, but occasionally he had access to communications facilities at his FOB (forward operating base). He called occasionally and was candid with me because I could relate to what he was doing. (He waited until he came home to tell his parents some things.) War contains periods of boredom punctuated by moments of terror. Berry had his share of both.

During one call he said, "Granddaddy, an IED hit my tank and seriously wounded the driver." (An IED is an improvised explosive device.)

"Wow!" I said. "Were you or anyone else hurt?"

"No," he responded. "I felt the blast but was not hurt."

"Was there a follow-up attack?"

"No," he said. "Not by them, and we didn't find anyone around. They set it off from a distance and got out of the area."

I sighed. "Berry, that is the advantage they have in a counterinsurgency situation. It happened to my unit in Vietnam numerous times. I'm just thankful you were not hurt. Stay safe."

During our next call I said, "Berry, someone sent me a new hood for a Honda. Got any idea who?"

He replied, "Sorry about that, Granddaddy. Hope you don't mind keeping it in your garage until I get back."

I retorted. "I will just put it on top of your car."

★★★

On January 10, 2005, Sandy's mother died. She went quietly in her sleep, and Sandy took her death hard. Sandy's family still did not know of my existence, so I attended the funeral incognito as Sally's escort. Although I could not be with Sandy at that difficult time, I hoped that my presence there supported her. While her mother's death was painful, it did relieve her of her caretaker responsibility and freed her to consider options for the future.

We began serious discussions about marriage. There were still complications.

"Sandy," I said. "Can we adjust to another relationship at this time in our lives? How will our children feel? I'm also concerned about our age difference."

She responded, "You may not be able to adjust to my slower, more deliberate way of doing things."

I echoed, "You may not be willing to give up the independence you have just obtained."

We concluded there were more reasons in favor of our marriage than against it.

Sandy told her husband she wanted a divorce. They could not agree on terms, so it became a contested divorce and dragged on into the summer of 2005.

Sandy's attorney advised her to avoid any relationship that subjected her to accusations of having another man in her life. Given her husband's long-time affair, I thought the advice was overkill. However, to protect Sandy, I cooperated. We were discreet about where we went together and with whom. We spent most of our together time at Sally's house, with Sally and Jack. Sally was a wonderful cook.

Sandy and I first visited Brian and Angie to tell them about our plans. At first Brian thought about his grandmother and then rebounded and said, "I just want what makes you happy."

Angie added, "Me too. I think you both will be happy, and we are happy for you."

We then went to see Marie and Brandon. After hearing my explanation, Marie asked "Then what will Sandy be to us?"

Sandy answered her, "Marie, I don't want to try to be a step-grandmother. I just want to be your friend."

I added, "No one will ever take the place of your grandmother in any of our hearts. But I know my life will be happier, and I hope Sandy's will be also."

Marie said "We are glad for both of you. You have my blessing." Brandon echoed her sentiments.

In June I flew to Fresno and visited Bill, Debbie, and Sara. I discussed Sandy and our relationship in detail and then said, "We plan to be married and would like to have your acceptance and hopefully your support."

Bill asked, "You are sure this is what you want?"

"Yes."

"Where will you live, her house or yours?" he asked.

"We will live in my house and turn it into our house."

He followed with, "Where will the wedding take place?"

I said, "Wynnbrook Church. It will be a small wedding; just a few close friends and family. Dr. Hicks will do the service. No reception following."

Debbie asked, "Have you both talked about how you may have to adjust to some aspects of each other's personality? You are so different from each other."

I responded, "Yes. We have talked about that a lot. We know what will be needed and think we can handle it. In the final analysis, the pros outweigh the cons."

Sara spoke up. "Sandy takes things slower than you do, Granddaddy. That may be good for you. I think you two will be happy."

"Bill," I said. "Sandy is a kind, loving Christian who is genuine. She is also sensitive to feelings you might have about her impact on any estate I might leave. So she is insisting on pre-nuptial agreements. She wants nothing from my estate."

Following our continued discussion, Debbie said "I certainly am supportive." Sara added, "Me too."

Bill said, "Perhaps Dr. Hicks would let me handle part of the service." With that, I felt better.

★★★

Soldiers serving in Iraq were given two weeks of R&R in the middle of their tour (just like Vietnam). Berry's turn came in September. While visiting his parents in Fresno, he developed a foot infection which prevented his return to combat duty. He was sent to his unit's rear detachment at Fort Benning until his foot healed. Once again my house became his home away from home. He and Sandy spent a lot of time together, and he was happy for us.

Sandy's divorce became effective on September 26 and we set our wedding date for November 26. Sandy's children were shocked when she told them. Three of her children did not want to meet me or come to the wedding. She blamed herself for not letting them know about me earlier. Her son David did agree to meet me. Sandy and I drove to Atlanta to spend the day with David and Megan. They were hospitable and receptive, expressing their happiness for us.

Sandra "Sandy" Ingram Cross, 2004.

At Berry's graduation from armor training: Fort Knox, 2004.

Sandy and me with Jack Brinkley and Sally Posey.

CHAPTER 22

My Territory Enlarged: 2005–2011

Sandy and I were married on November 26, 2005, at Wynnbrook Baptist Church. Our pastor, Dr. Brad Hicks, and my son, Dr. Bill Steele performed the ceremony. Sally Posey and Jack Brinkley, along with Elsie and David Bickley, stood with us. When I noticed Sandy crying, I turned around to see her son David and his wife entering the church. My entire family attended, too. (Berry was still at Fort Benning for treatment for his foot infection but was mobile and able to attend.) Brandon took photos while Sara organized the group shots.

Sandy was a beautiful, radiant bride. She wore a white dress and a pretty smile and held a bouquet of red carnations.

Bill began the ceremony by saying, "I am pleased to be able to take part in this ceremony which is so meaningful at this point in my dad's life."

I was filled with happiness at those words.

We honeymooned at the beach house in Florida and had a wonderful time. We returned to Columbus to live in what was now our house.

Not long after our return to Columbus, Sandy's unmarried son, Kevin, went to lunch with us, and we became acquainted. He realized we could become friends, and that I posed no threat to his close relationship with his mother. One more relationship hurdle had been overcome.

Our Sunday school teacher, retired Army Colonel John Latimer, worked at Total Systems and knew Sandy's son Brad and his wife Elisa, who also worked there. John put their minds at ease about me which provided an opportunity to meet them for lunch one day. We began a friendship that has grown close over the ensuing years.

I overcame the last relationship hurdle in late December. Sandy saved some of her furniture for her daughter Leslie. She could not get the items, however, until she and her family came to Columbus over the Christmas holidays. We met then and connected right away. She and her husband David were friendly to me and we discovered many common interests.

I breathed a sigh of relief. My relationship with Sandy's children and grandchildren was going to be fine.

My territory of friends has enlarged since God brought Sandy into my life. In addition to her family, her numerous friends from grade school to the present have welcomed me into their world. Similarly, I have introduced Sandy to my army family and she has joined me at Wynnbrook Baptist Church.

Sandy's grandchild, Mia, was born on April 10. Mia was David's daughter and the first member of Sandy's family that I will have known from the outset.

Without trying to interject ourselves into each other's family, Sandy and I wanted to treat everyone as family. We made the beach house available to Sandy's family in addition to my family. We seized the opportunity to be there with them as much as possible. We especially enjoyed seeing the children appreciate Venture Out.

In July 2006 Sandy and I flew to California to visit Bill and his family and to help Debbie celebrate receiving her doctorate in psychology. She finished the required course work prior to leaving Louisiana and completed her dissertation in Fresno. They showed us around the Fresno area, and we explored Yosemite National Park—a beautiful area. While there, everyone got to know and appreciate Sandy. She had never been to California. Therefore, we spent a week exploring along the coast from Los Angeles to Monterey and San Francisco. Hollywood was a big disappointment for Sandy. She had expected glamour but instead it was rather sleazy.

One of my goals was to get all of my grandchildren together as often as possible so that they could build on their relationships. When someone suggested that we rendezvous at the beach house for a weekend in September, I leapt at the idea. Sara was not there, but Berry drove from Louisiana to join us. He was attending college in Hammond. We had a marvelous time. They stayed up late talking, and it reminded me of the evenings spent with Ginny's brothers and sisters on visits home. On Saturday afternoon, we went out on the Gulf on a charter fishing boat. It was big enough for all of us to fish plus it had an air-conditioned cabin for me when I needed a break.

We left the pier around 2 p.m., but it was pleasant due to the time of year and a slightly overcast sky. We were all in good spirits. We could see the backside of Venture Out as we moved out through the bay and Marie commented, "We have had lots of good times down here. I always looked forward to a weekend at the beach."

Brian added "Yes, and Grandmother would always boil shrimp."

As we went through the jetty and into the Gulf, some dolphins came up to check us out and everyone rushed to the side to get a look. Before long, the captain eased back on the throttle and said, "Get ready to fish. The sonar shows a school of fish just ahead. It may be Amberjack." The rods had already been set out; now the bait was quickly snagged onto hooks and the lines played out at an appropriate distance.

Brian was the first. "I got one!" he yelled.

While he was reeling his in, Brandon's rod began to dip. "Me too! Both of them brought in a good-sized Amberjack. While they fished, I watched and took pictures. Everyone caught one or more, and we took a group photo with the catch when we got back to the pier that evening.

Angie suggested, "Why don't we make this an annual event?"

I replied, "Good idea! I am all for it, if we can get everyone together."

The next month, Sandy decided to do something about the pain in her hips. She had her first hip replaced in October, and the second in January 2007. According to her, it was like getting a new pair of hips.

In an effort to give Sandy some relaxation following her second hip joint replacement, I planned a twelve-day cruise to several Caribbean Islands in early spring. I knew she usually got motion sickness, but I figured the Caribbean would be relatively calm. She could also start on a motion sickness prevention program prior to departure.

We had a nice drive to Tampa and enjoyed the city on the day we arrived. We boarded the ship the following day, and as we were going to dinner, she said, "The ship is moving." We reached our assigned table and introduced ourselves. I noticed that Sandy was uncharacteristically quiet. The salad arrived and Sandy leaned over to me and said "I can't eat or I will be sick." We returned to our cabin.

The ship's doctor gave me several things for her but getting off the ship appeared to be the only solution. The first stop occurred on the third day at Grand Turk Island. It had an airport, and we could fly back to Tampa. The respite I planned had turned out to be an ordeal for Sandy. I am sure that she was apprehensive but wanted to try it for me.

Our lives were focusing more and more on family, friends, and church. We celebrated birthdays, with lunch or dinner, for each family member except those located in California. Fortunately, I was able to see my local grandchildren and their spouses often.

After trying several different occupations, Brian found his niche working for the East Alabama Cable Company in Phenix City. He had a good grasp of things mechanical and liked being outdoors, working alone. He was self-motivated, dependable, and required little supervi -

sion. Angie was still successful working for Aflac as a life insurance underwriting assistant.

Marie was working at the Morgan Keegan stock brokerage office in Columbus. She and I met for lunch occasionally. She had an outgoing personality, was good with numbers, and did not mind work. Brandon was the senior technician at the automotive shop where he worked in Opelika, Alabama. He demonstrated integrity and dependability—he and Marie have made a good team.

Although both families had delayed having children (waiting for their finances to improve), Marie and Brandon decided they had waited long enough. Marie's due date was in July 2007. It must have been catching, because Brian and Angie soon announced they were expecting a baby in September 2007. Needless to say, those were happy announcements for me.

In July we met Bill and his family at Dollywood. We drove there and enjoyed the scenery on the way. We enjoyed being with them, but Dollywood was very crowded and traffic moved slowly during show times. The important thing was that we got to be with them.

In July and September, the Steele family was blessed with the birth of two little girls. Elise Shannon Culpepper was born on July 31 and Grace Virginia Steele on September 26. God was good! I could spend time with my two great-grandchildren—perhaps even more than I did with my grandchildren when they were very young.

Berry called from Hammond in November. He wanted us to meet his girlfriend, Danielle, over the Thanksgiving break. They had met at a Christian youth center in Hammond. We were delighted.

However, over the Thanksgiving weekend, we began to have misgivings. Danielle's personality seemed to move from one extreme to another, and we thought Berry needed to think carefully about a relationship with her. They were planning to get married in January, but Bill and Debbie urged Berry to wait at least until August. Berry remained optimistic and they got married in January anyway.

Nine months later, they separated. It took Berry a long time to accept this and deal with Danielle's departure. He started working in restaurants and did not return to college.

The year 2008 proved very busy for Sandy and me. We both had health issues. I had problems with arthritis in my knees and one foot (too many road marches), as well as frequent skin cancer problems (too much time in the sun). Sandy had cataracts removed from both eyes and received lens implants.

Marie called me one day and asked about the possibility of Elise being dedicated at Wynnbrook Church. I was elated. I had been hoping that she and Brandon would start going to church and join us at Wynnbrook. Arrangements were made, and Elise was dedicated on Mother's Day.

Bill visited us in early August, and we all went to the beach house together. Later that month, Sandy and I attended an American Idol concert. We immediately realized the concert was not for our age group.

Wally Veaudry, my long time army buddy, died that summer and it was very sad for me. We went through a lot together, professionally and personally. Wally had been suffering with lung cancer for a year. Surprisingly enough, he had never smoked. Wally's two daughters and I were with him the night he passed away. I was blessed to be able to help his girls with the funeral arrangements and give his eulogy.

In October Bill accepted a call to become pastor of the Sierra Heights Baptist Church in Fresno. But he was still able to come to Columbus with his family between Christmas and New Year's Day. It was a nice way for us to end 2008.

★★★

For years Sandy and I had hoped that Jack and Sally would marry. We knew they were suited for each other and cared for each other. Sally was ready, but Jack had trouble making the decision. I decided to try to convince him to take the next step.

When we went to dinner together on Valentine's Day in 2009, I said to Jack while he was driving, "Jack. Sandy and I love the both of you, and we want you and Sally to be as happy as we are. We know that you love Sally and that she loves you. It is time you asked her to marry you—time is passing."

Jack made a wrong turn and almost caused us to get hit by another car. We have laughed about that event many times. But it worked. Sally and Jack were married on May 25, 2009.

Sandy's sister-in-law, Kay, also married in May in Tallahassee, Florida. We attended the wedding. Sandy had some sad moments thinking of her late brother, but she did everything she could to help Kay have a happy day.

2009 turned out to be a traumatic year for Sandy. David's wife, Megan, initiated divorce proceedings. Sandy devoted a lot of her time and energy helping David adjust to the situation. He moved to Columbus to live with his brother Kevin and got a job managing a local restaurant. David had Mia on weekends, but Sandy agreed to keep her with us on Saturday nights while he worked. Mia went to church with us on Sundays.

Since Bill was coming to Columbus for Christmas, I suggested to our pastor Kevin Calhoun that he might like a Sunday off and Bill could take his place. Kevin and Bill agreed. To hear my son preach in our church was a dream come true. He brought us a memorable message and delivered it in an outstanding manner.

At a luncheon for family and close friends following the service, everyone echoed my feelings.

"I enjoyed Bill's message." "What a great sermon." "He is such a good speaker." "I know you are proud of him."

Afterward, I told Bill, "I have never been more proud of you. I think your mother also heard you and feels the same way."

When 2010 rolled around, Dr. Steve Beaty and I decided it was time to have my cataracts removed. I wanted him to do it before he left for a month-long mission trip to Zimbabwe, Africa. Sandy had benefited from such surgery, and I was anxious to improve my vision. One eye was done in March followed by the other in April. We went to the beach house for my recuperation.

Bill suggested we meet in Branson for a few days in May. Sandy and I drove there leisurely. Bill, Debbie, and Sara flew to New Orleans, picked up Berry, and arrived in Branson shortly after we did. Over dinner at the hotel, we discussed what to do. Looking at the schedule of shows and activities, I said, "Sandy you might like the show with impersonations of famous singers."

She replied, "Maybe, but this one sounds good also. It has songs from all the great Broadway plays."

Debbie pitched in with, "I have heard that the Chinese acrobats are super."

Sara put forth her suggestion. "We should try the zip line and canopy. They hook you to a cable and you slide from tree to tree."

I responded, "Sandy and I will sit that one out!"

Berry said, "Anything is fine with me."

Bill got to the point. "Right now, let's decide on something to do tonight." All the shows turned out to be great and the zip line and canopy was a winner for those four who tried it.

One afternoon while the girls were shopping and Berry was napping, Bill and I had some quality time together at the hotel restaurant over coffee. During our discussion, I said, "Bill, I value the time we have together. I feel like we have grown closer over the past few years, and I would like for us to get together whenever we can find the time."

"I feel the same way," he responded. "We need to make it happen."

"Let's try to do so at least twice a year," I said. "You can come to Columbus, I will go to Fresno, or we can meet somewhere else like we are doing now."

"Good," he responded, "I will try to be in Columbus for the Christmas holidays."

On the way home, I commented to Sandy, "This was a great trip! I especially enjoyed my time with Bill. Perhaps I am closing the gap that resulted from all my time away from home."

The long trip back to Columbus also provided quality time for Sandy and me. She was such a positive impact on my life, and I wanted to make sure she knew it.

"Sandy. You have helped me in many ways, probably more than you know. You have certainly gotten me to slow down and taught me how to live a relaxed, casual, slower way of life."

"Really," she said. "I'm so glad."

"Yes, really. You convinced me that we could arrive somewhere on time, rather than five minutes early, or even be late without causing a problem. You let me know that people no longer pressed their jeans, that I could go to the grocery store without a jacket, and that I could wear shorts on hot days. I joke that you are damaging my image. But in fact you are helping me live happier and longer!"

"That's my goal," she said. "To make you live longer."

I was enjoying my new life. I was extremely pleased to see my grandchildren developing into great parents and enjoying the responsibility. Marie and Brandon took advantage of the decline in the housing market to purchase a house in Smiths, Alabama. Brian and Angie decided to rent or sell their house and move into the Phenix City house vacated by his sister. Brian and Angie also joined Wynnbrook and had Grace confirmed on October 17. Now we all worship at the same place, and I look forward to Sundays with added enthusiasm.

Both great-granddaughters were growing fast and their personalities were developing. They were in day care centers, so I could visit or take them for outings. They were both loving but very different. Grace was taller than Elise, had curly chestnut hair, dark blue eyes, and a very outgoing personality. Elise was petite, with light hair, light blue eyes, and a quiet personality. Both were smart and likeable. They ran to me whenever they saw me coming. I braced myself and enjoyed their hugs.

Bill and his family spent a few days with us during Christmas 2010. We drove to Dooly County to look at the farm, stop by the cemetery, and visit with Shannon Akin and his wife, Grace.

Bill suggested to Shannon, "We are coming back to visit next summer, and I wondered if you might consider having a reunion of the Akin family at your lodge sometime while we are here. It is an ideal place for such a gathering, and we have not gotten together in years."

To our delight, Shannon replied. "It would be nice to see everyone again. I would be glad to." Sixty members of the Akin family attended a reunion on July 9. Libby's son Doug brought his family all the way from Washington state. My entire family was there. Bill spent time with his cousins, grandchildren became acquainted, and my great-grandchildren had a wonderful time running around—inside and outside. After lunch, the head of each family introduced his or her group, and we took lots of pictures. I was somewhat concerned about being with a large gathering of Ginny's family with someone else by my side. My concern quickly dissipated, however, when I saw Ginny's family welcome Sandy and express their happiness for us.

Aflac also had a reunion in 2011. The corporation held its annual breakfast for retirees to update them and thank them for their service. I was unable to attend the event and missed seeing everyone. I still had some very close retired Aflac friends and enjoyed catching up with them whenever possible.

The bond among military retirees, however, is stronger than among civilian retirees. I am firmly connected to the Army. Fort Benning conducts annual retiree gatherings, and I am invited to attend conferences, social functions, and ceremonies throughout the year. "Once a soldier, always a soldier" could be one of my grandmother's memory phrases. Although retired from the Army for thirty-one years, I still feel a special bond every time I am among soldiers.

Soldiers have kept the United States free. Today, it is a bastion of freedom because its young men and women have answered the call to defend its liberties over the past two centuries. I have them to thank for the wonderful life opportunities I have had. Will future generations have that opportunity? Recently, I gained some insight into the answer.

I was attending a graduation ceremony for a company of young men finishing Basic and Advanced Infantry Training. The day was warm and sunny with a breeze moving the flags slightly. The band played a stirring march tune as the troops came up on line. The men in formation were sharp, standing tall and still while the speaker delivered his remarks. When the order was given to "pass in review," the band began marching, and the lead unit turned sharply behind it. As each rank marched past the reviewing stand and turned their heads to the right in arrow straight lines, I saw the proud, determined look in the eyes of those strong young men that must have been in the eyes of the thousands who marched before them. I thought, *Yes, America's freedom is still in good hands!*

Our wedding, November 26, 2005.
First row: Me and Sandy;
second row: Angie, Brian, and Sara;
third row: Bill, Berry, Debbie, Marie, and Brandon.

Berry in Iraq, 2005.

Sara, 2010.

Bill and his family, 2010.

Brian and his family, 2010.

Grace Virginia Steele, age 3.

Marie and her family, 2010.

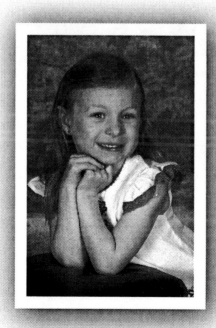

Elise Shannon Culpepper, age 3.

My family in 2009 from L to R. First row: Sara, Marie, and Debbie; second row: Sandy, Angie, Grace, Brandon, and Elise; third row: Bill, me, Brian, and Berry.

Sandy's family on her birthday in June 2011 from L to R. First row: Brooks, Thomas, Katharine, Mia, and Samuel; second row: Elisa, Leslie, Sandy, and Kevin; third row: Brad, David (Suarez), Bradley, and David (Cross).

Two happy people—Sandy and me!

Epilogue: 2012

I never dreamed that life would be a stimulating, rewarding, loving, and happy experience in my 80s. God has blessed me with the physical and mental ability to stay active and enjoy life. He has also blessed me with positive reinforcement from those I love and worked with.

I was elected President of the National Infantry Association in 2011 (a non-salaried position). The Association's mission is to support infantry programs and recognize infantrymen for their service. It has an office with a staff of three located in the National Infantry Museum Building near Fort Benning. My involvement is minimal (a few days each month), but it necessitates more frequent attendance at various Fort Benning functions and ceremonies. Sandy accompanies me to some of these functions. She has gained an appreciation for the patriotism of soldiers and the ties that bind us together.

Sandy is a delightful, sensitive, loving, and caring woman. I love her deeply and want to share the rest of my life with her. My love for her family continues to grow as well.

My son and his wife Debbie are healthy, enjoy their work, and are happy together. Bill is a smart, considerate, caring man who tries to "practice what he preaches." Debbie is an energetic, perceptive, hardworking person who cares for her family. They are both active individuals and enjoy living in California. They run, bike, play tennis, swim, sail, water ski, and snow ski almost year-round. Debbie participates in state-wide tennis competitions, is a professor with a local college, and is a counselor. Bill enjoys his church family, and they love him.

Sara attends college at the University of California at Los Angeles (UCLA) and works part-time. She is a bright, pretty, very personable young woman interested in becoming a doctor. (Perhaps one day I will have a doctor in the family who can write a prescription for me!) However, if she decides to become something else that is fine. She will do well in any field she chooses. I just want her to have a full and happy life.

Berry is now in Fresno living with his parents, attending college, and working at a restaurant. Berry is a kind, considerate, handsome young man with lots of ability. He needs only to set some goals and apply himself. I have faith that he will do so.

Brian and Angie are happy together and are providing a loving home for Grace. Brian enjoys Alabama football games, guns, and auto racing. He checks on me often and is always ready to help me do things I shouldn't be doing now (like climbing ladders). Angie and I communicate frequently via email and she sends pictures of Grace.

Marie and Brandon are great parents, too. Elise is benefiting from the way they are teaching and helping her grow. Marie and I chat on the phone and text each other often. She sends me pictures of Elise via texts. Brandon is a good, hard-working, dependable man and a firm but kind and gentle father.

Sandy's granddaughter, Mia, is smart, lovable, and a very perceptive little girl. She is benefiting from being around her grandmother on weekends. She already reflects many of Sandy's mannerisms and often reacts to situations like Sandy does. In many ways, she is Sandy's clone. It reminds me of how much I gleaned from my grandmother many years ago when I used to follow her around the kitchen listening to her words of wisdom.

My life has been full, interesting, enjoyable, and long. But there is something else a man longs for. Unfortunately, most do not realize it until late in life when there is more time for reflection. That "something" is the belief that you have done your very best with what God gave you. Everything depends upon the choices you make and the priorities you set as you go through life's journey.

In retrospect, I believe that I did well in my military career and later in my business life with Aflac. I believe that I made a contribution to both endeavors and, hopefully, had a positive influence on people along the way.

Overall, have I been a good man and a decent person? That is for others to judge, but I like to think so.

However, there are choices and priorities that haunt me. I should have devoted more time and effort to my family. I should have provided for more quality time, especially for the boys. I should have spent more time with my parents in their last few years when I was in closer proximity to them. I often wonder if I could have done more to help Wade develop greater self-esteem and confidence. What more could I have done to help him overcome his alcohol addiction? Should I have done more to provide a positive influence for his children? I have also wrestled mightily with what else I could have done to make Ginny's last few years easier. Finally, and probably central to all of the foregoing, was how late in life I brought God completely into my heart.

Yes, I have had a wonderful journey through life. But, oh how much more beneficial and satisfying it could have been, had I developed a closer, personal relationship with my Savior earlier in my lifetime! I pray that those who follow will benefit from my experience.

Acknowledgments

First I want to acknowledge my late wife Virginia "Ginny" Akin Steele, who shared much of my journey and contributed so much to it. She had a large role in my life and was much loved and appreciated. She even contributed to this book because I used her notes with important family dates to help me remember. I also want to acknowledge my late son Wade—I am sorry his life was so short and that I could not have done more to make it longer and happier.

Many wonderful people were important in my journey and mentioned in my book: boyhood friends, schoolmates, fellow soldiers, and co-workers. I owe them all for being there with me, both in and out of the Army. I am especially grateful and indebted to those courageous men in the 5th Mech Battalion who were wounded or made the supreme sacrifice while I was their commander. They fought well, and I pray that those who died rest in peace.

Also very helpful in gathering and confirming information were my son Bill Jr. and his wife Debbie, my grandson Brian and his wife Angie, my granddaughter Marie and her husband Brandon, my grandson Berry, my granddaughter Sara, and Brenda Ellis.

I was fortunate to find a wonderful editor—Lorraine Fico-White of Magnifico Manuscripts—to help in the presentation of what I wanted to tell. Her assistance was invaluable. She quickly saw what needed to be changed, added, or eliminated to improve the manuscript's readability, flow, and interest, and she tactfully influenced me to agree. She deftly guided me through the process and stayed with it until everything was accomplished and grammatically correct. She is extremely professional. I enjoyed working with her and I owe her a debt of gratitude.

Jim Gates, one of my wife's schoolmates and now a friend of mine, provided valuable assistance when I was getting the photos together for use with the book. His help is most appreciated.

Shannon E. Coffey of Artifacts Studio designed and provided the layout of the cover and the book and was responsible for the restoration and prepress of the images. She also assisted in the development of the family tree charts. She is very creative, highly proficient, and I appreciated her help. The cover photo of the 22nd Infantry Regimental Crest was provided by the courtesy of her father, Robert Coffey II.

Finally, I want to acknowledge the help of my wife Sandy Cross Steele. She was so kind and considerate in giving me quiet, undisturbed time during the many hours I spent focused in front of the computer in the writing process. Also appreciated was the time and effort she put into reading my drafts and giving me helpful comments. Most of all, I thank her for being in my life and making every day a wonderful experience.

APPENDIX A:

Glossary

Adjutant. Another name for the staff officer (S-1) who handles personnel and administrative matters for a battalion or regiment. *See also S-1.*

Air Medal. Medal awarded for meritorious achievement while participating in aerial flight. (Awarded eighteen for my involvement in the command and control of land combat operations in Vietnam.)

All-Volunteer Army. The U.S. Army following the cessation of the draft in the early 1970s where all soldiers were recruited—not drafted.

AO. An abbreviation for area of operations. A geographical area in which a unit is directed to operate. It is usually delineated by recognizable terrain features such as roads, rivers, and land masses.

APC. An abbreviation for armored personnel carrier. Armored vehicles that move on revolving metal tracks. Designed to transport infantrymen in the battle area while providing protection from small arms fire and shrapnel. APCs are vulnerable to anti-tank weapons such as RPGs. *See also M113 APC, RPG.*

Armed Forces Honor Medal. Medal awarded by the Republic of Vietnam for contributions to the organization and training of the Vietnamese military. (Awarded for my service while a battalion commander in Vietnam.)

Armed Forces Staff College. Schooling for selected officers of all U.S. military services for duty involving joint operations. Currently named Joint Forces Staff College.

Armored Personnel Carrier. *See APC.*

Army. The ready, active Army force. *See also regular Army; U.S. Army.*

Army Commendation Medal. Medal awarded for meritorious achievement or meritorious service. (I received three. One for meritorious service with the U.S. Army Training Mission in Saudi Arabia; one for meritorious service with the Infantry Branch office in Washington D.C.; and one for achievement with the 9th Infantry Division Forward Command Post in Vietnam.)

Army Reserve. Army personnel not on active duty but available as individuals or part of a unit for call to active duty if needed. *See also U.S. Army Reserve.*

Artillery. Indirect fire weapons providing overhead fire against enemy targets. Can also be used in direct fire role.

Barracks. Structures in which troops are housed.

Basic Airborne Course. A course offered at the Infantry School at Fort Benning designed to train soldiers to parachute in combat conditions.

Battalion. Military unit composed of two or more company-sized units (usually four or five) with an approximate total of 800 troops.

Battery. An artillery unit comparable in size to a company and usually organized around six large, indirect fire weapons called howitzers.

Brigade. Military unit composed of two or more battalions with about 3,000 troops.

Bronze Star. A medal awarded for heroic or meritorious achievement or service. (I received two. One (with a V device for valor) for actions during an engagement near Cai Lay, Vietnam in September 1967 and one for achievement during the Tet Offensive in February 1968.)

CGSC. Abbreviation for the Command and General Staff Course offered at the U.S. Army Command and General Staff College at Fort Leavenworth, Kansas. The course is designed to prepare army officers for command and staff duty at division and higher levels. Currently named the Command and General Staff School (CGSS).

Cantonment. An area built up for troop units such as a camp, post, or station.

Civil Action Honor Medal. Medal awarded by the government of the Republic of Vietnam for significant contributions to civic actions. (Awarded for civic actions carried out under my direction while serving in Vietnam.)

Combat Infantry Badge. Badge awarded to a member of a brigade-sized infantry unit (or smaller) during any period the unit was engaged in active combat.

Commissary. Military facility on post comparable to a grocery store and used by soldiers and their dependents.

Company. Military unit usually composed of four or five platoon-sized units with an approximate total of 200 troops. Examples of a company include rifle company, tank company, and headquarters company.

Distinguished Flying Cross. Medal for heroism while participating in aerial flight. (Awarded for my actions during an engagement near Cai Lay in February 1968.)

Distinguished Service Medal. Medal for exceptionally meritorious service in a duty of great responsibility. (Awarded for my service in several assignments from July 1971 to December 1978.)

Distinguished Service Cross. Medal for extraordinary heroism while engaged in combat. It is the second highest award for bravery. (Awarded to Lieutenant Lee Alley for his actions during the defense of FSB Cudgel.)

Division. Military organization composed of several regiments or brigades and separate battalions with 15,000 to 18,000 troops.

FOB. Abbreviation for forward operating base. A base of operation in a secure but temporary position where a unit functions in a somewhat exposed position relative to the enemy.

FSA. Abbreviation for Farm Security Administration. Federal government agency established during the Great Depression to provide financial aid and other assistance to the farming sector.

FSB. Abbreviation for fire support base. A unit (usually artillery) is set up to provide supporting fires in this area. It is normally defended by an infantry unit.

G-1. Staff officer of a division, corps, or Army responsible for personnel and administrative matters within the command.

Gallantry Cross with Palm. Medal awarded by the government of the Republic of Vietnam for gallantry in action against an armed enemy. (Awarded for my actions as battalion commander during the Tet Offensive.)

Garrison. Personnel occupying an army post, camp, or station.

IOBC. Abbreviation for the Infantry Officer's Basic Course offered at the U.S. Army Infantry School at Fort Benning. The course is designed to train newly commissioned infantry officers for company-level duty. Currently named the Infantry Basic Officer Leader's Course (IBOLC).

IOAC. Abbreviation for the Infantry Officer's Advanced Course offered at the U.S. Army Infantry School at Fort Benning. The course is designed to train infantry captains for command and staff work at battalion and brigade levels. Currently named the Maneuver Captain's Career Course (MCCC).

Infantry. Soldiers who are specifically trained for the role of fighting on foot to engage in close combat and kill or destroy the enemy. They have historically borne the brunt of the casualties of combat in wars. Infantry is the only branch capable of seizing and holding ground.

Infantry Insignia. First authorized in 1875, this symbol of two crossed muskets is worn by personnel of the U.S. Army Infantry.

J-1. Staff officer of a joint command responsible for personnel and administrative matters within the command.

Legion of Merit. Medal awarded for exceptionally meritorious conduct in the performance of outstanding services. (I received two. One for my service in Vietnam and one for my service while executive officer and senior aide to the Army Chief of Staff.)

M113 APC. (M113 military armored personnel carriers.) These tracked vehicles were used in World War II and Vietnam but are now replaced with the Bradley fighting vehicle, a much improved armored personnel carrier. *See also armored personnel carrier.*

Mechanized. A unit that is equipped with armored vehicles such as Armored Personnel Carriers. *See also armored personnel carrier.*

Medal of Honor. Medal given to a soldier who risked his or her life above and beyond the call of duty while engaged in combat. It is the highest award for bravery. (Lieutenant Lee Alley was recommended for this award.)

Meritorious Service Medal. Medal awarded for outstanding meritorious achievement or service. (Awarded for my service with the U.S. Army Leadership Board April–July 1971.)

NATO. Abbreviation for the North Atlantic Treaty Organization. An organization set up after World War II to provide for the common defense of the member states.

NCOs. Abbreviation for non-commissioned officers. Enlisted men designated as officers but not commissioned by an act of Congress.

NCSC. Abbreviation for the Naval Command and Staff Course offered at the U.S. Navy War College in Newport, Rhode Island. The course is designed to prepare naval officers for increased responsibilities as commanders and captains. It is also attended by selected officers from other services. The course is currently separated into two courses taught in two separate schools: the Naval Command College and the Naval Staff College.

National Guard. Military units under the control of individual states. They can be called together and brought on duty by the state or the federal government in time of need. Often referred to as militia.

Platoon. Military unit made up of several smaller units (squads) with about forty personnel. *See also squad.*

Post. A more permanent army installation than a camp or a station.

Post Exchange. Military retail facility located on post for use by military personnel and their dependents. It is comparable to a small Wal-Mart.

Regiment. A military unit (comparable to a brigade) composed of two or more battalions, usually with about 3,000 troops. *See also brigade.*

Regimental Crest. The crest is worn on the epaulets of soldiers of the 22nd Infantry Regiment. The white and blue shield symbolizes the colors of the old and new infantry. The bundle of five arrows represents the five American Indian wars. The face on the sun represents the Spanish-American War. The shield is divided by a partitioned line of embattlements (representing wars in which the regiment participated).

Regular Army. Another name for the active U.S. Army. *See also Army; U.S. Army.*

RPG. Abbreviation for a rocket-propelled grenade. It is a man-portable, shoulder-fired, high-explosive, anti-tank rocket.

ROTC. Abbreviation for Reserve Officer Training Program. It is a program designed to train high school and college students to become commissioned officers in the armed services.

S-1. Staff officer at battalion or brigade level responsible for personnel and administrative matters within the unit. *See also adjutant.*

S-2. Staff officer at battalion or brigade level responsible for enemy intelligence gathering and analysis.

Senior Parachutist Badge. Badge awarded to personnel making a minimum of 30 jumps, including 2 mass jumps and 2 night jumps.

Silver Star. Medal awarded for gallantry in action against an enemy of the United States while involved in combat. (I received two. One for actions in the Plain of Reeds and another for actions during the defense of FSB Cudgel in November 1967.)

Squad. A small army unit of approximately nine personnel. Three or four squads make up one platoon. *See also platoon.*

Tactical Command Post. The location of the command element of a unit while the unit is involved in tactical operations.

USAIS. Abbreviation for the U.S. Army Infantry School in Fort Benning, Georgia. Currently named U.S. Army Maneuver Center of Excellence.

U.S. Army. The active Army. *See also Army, regular Army.*

U.S. Army Reserve. Army personnel not on active duty but available as individuals or part of a unit for call to active duty if needed. *See also Army Reserve.*

U.S. Army War College. Schooling for selected officers in the grades of colonel or lieutenant colonel. Located at Carlisle Barracks, Pennsylvania, this college provides instruction on leadership, strategy, and joint-service/international operations.

APPENDIX B: Family Trees
Steele Family Tree

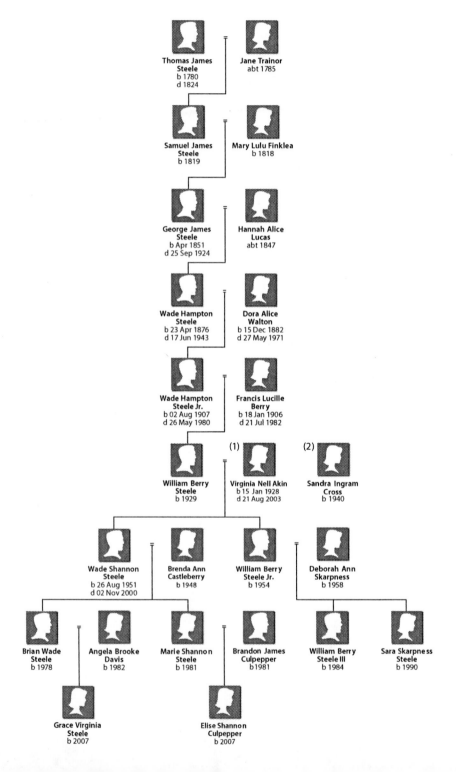

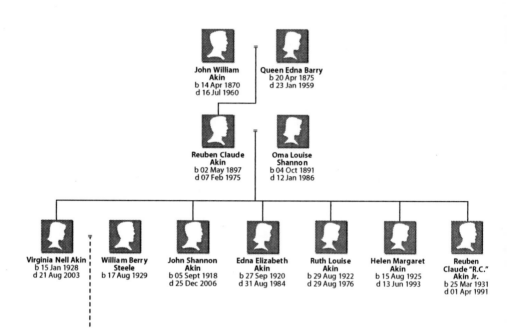

John William Akin
b 14 Apr 1870
d 16 Jul 1960

Queen Edna Barry
b 20 Apr 1875
d 23 Jan 1959

Reuben Claude Akin
b 02 May 1897
d 07 Feb 1975

Oma Louise Shannon
b 04 Oct 1891
d 12 Jan 1986

Virginia Nell Akin
b 15 Jan 1928
d 21 Aug 2003

William Berry Steele
b 17 Aug 1929

John Shannon Akin
b 05 Sept 1918
d 25 Dec 2006

Edna Elizabeth Akin
b 27 Sep 1920
d 31 Aug 1984

Ruth Louise Akin
b 29 Aug 1922
d 29 Aug 1976

Helen Margaret Akin
b 15 Aug 1925
d 13 Jun 1993

Reuben Claude "R.C." Akin Jr.
b 25 Mar 1931
d 01 Apr 1991

(previous page)

NOTE: Family information courtesy of the family and Ancestry.com.